Who Am I? Who Are You?

Who Am I? Who Are You?

Coping with Friends,
Feelings &
Other Teenage Dilemmas

Kathleen London with Frank Caparulo

Letters and Introduction by Beth Winship

Addison-Wesley Publishing Company
Reading, Massachusetts • Menlo Park, California • London
Amsterdam • Don Mills, Ontario • Sydney

Library of Congress Cataloging in Publication Data

London, Kathleen.
  Who am I? Who are you?

  1. Adolescent psychology.   2. Emotions.
3. Interpersonal relations.   I. Caparulo, Frank.
II. Title.
BF724.3.E5L66   1983   155.5   83-2828
ISBN 0-201-10813-5

ISBN 0-201-10813-5

ABCDEFGHIJ-DO-8543

Cover design and photograph by Marshall Henrichs
Text design by Jennie Ray Bush/Designworks, Cambridge, MA
Drawings by Marci Davis, Cambridge, MA
Set in 10-point ITC Bookman Light by P & M Typesetting, Inc.,
  Waterbury, CT

To Tina and Jeffer for putting up with Mom,
to Shannon for sharing her thoughts and feelings,
and to Dubie and Terry for just being around,
with love.

K.L.

Contents

Who Am I? Who Are You?

Introduction

Adolescence is a topsy-turvy time. Suddenly, strong feelings seem to pull you this way and that. Sometimes you want to scream at your parents. Sometimes you want to kill your little brother. Sometimes you feel so happy you could fly. Sometimes you are so full of love you could melt.

The strength of these feelings may scare you. Kids from all over the country write letters to my newspaper column, "Ask Beth," wanting to know about their emotions. They tell me: "I love this guy so much I could die." "I hate this creep in my class." "I feel so angry . . . frightened . . . delirious . . . green with envy." Kids wonder if it is okay to have such strong feelings. They wonder if other people have them, too; or are they the only ones to feel a certain way?

The answer is that everyone experiences these emotions at one time or another. A wide range and variety of emotions is inevitable—human—and emotions can be beneficial, so long as you learn how to express them productively.

This book was written to help kids understand their feelings. The authors have had years of experience with young people, as parents, teachers, counselors, and authors of books for and about young people. They explain clearly what emotions are, how they make you feel, and how to express them sensibly and usefully. Sample letters, taken from those I've received, show how other kids have felt under circumstances that occur in everyday life. Perhaps you have been in the same boat and had similar feelings, or have friends or family going through similar experiences.

An emotion is a feeling or sensation that you experience in response to something or someone. Emotions are different from intellectual thoughts or physical reactions, yet you cannot separate how you feel from your mind or body. When you feel love for someone, you may think something very logical ("Where is the best place for us to have lunch together?") and at the same time experience physiological changes, such as an increased heartbeat or sweaty palms.

Emotions can involve another person, a piece of music, an animal, a bird call, a building, an accident, or a lake—almost anything that has meaning for you. If the emotion is minor, it will arouse a small physical response, perhaps a smile or frown. If it is more important to you, it will involve more action, perhaps a leap, a yell, or a sense of tensing up.

Emotions developed way back when humans were first evolving. Some of the physical reactions to emotions are not very appropriate any more. When danger meant a saber-toothed tiger about to attack, the physical reaction of fear prepared prehistoric people for vigorous action—to fight or run away. Danger to you is more likely to be something like a major math test, a piano recital, or an important game. Fighting or fleeing are usually not sensible responses. But that physical reaction (the surge of adrenalin that prepares you for violent action) still goes on. That is why it is so important for you to learn to channel this energy in appropriate ways. Otherwise it sets you up for inappropriate action, such as yelling at someone for no real reason, or swatting your little brother.

Other situations produce emotions with physical responses that are still useful. The tenderness we feel when we see a little baby, for example, sets up the desire to care for the child. The anxiety we feel when we are alone on a dark, deserted street helps us to be cautious and careful.

One of the most important aspects of emotional maturity is learning to recognize what you're feeling and to express yourself, rather than trying to ignore or hide the feeling. Strong reactions have to have some place to go. Hiding feelings is like putting your finger over the top of a bottle of soda. If you shake it, it will explode. When emotions shake you up inside, you have to learn to "let off steam" or "take the cork off" them, or they will burst out, too.

Being open about feelings is often a problem for adolescents. Many teenagers like to be cool. They don't want to appear silly or vulnerable. They write me that they are smiling on the outside, but crying on the inside. In fact, many of you become so expert at hiding your emotions that you even deny you have any feelings.

One reason teenagers fear to show their emotions is that adolescence is a very self-conscious time. You are just trying to figure out who you are and you are supercritical of yourselves and of each other, too. You worry that if you act emotional other kids may make fun of you, or think you're babyish. Many kids get the idea that being too sad or happy or angry in front of someone else will cause them to lose status. People, especially young people, do tend to point the finger and jeer at those who act in an excessive or flamboyant way. So young people bottle up their feelings or bury them deep within and try to act as if nothing affects them.

Another reason kids try to act cool is that they fear losing control. They believe that if they let their anger rise to the surface, they might actually strike someone or break something. Learning self-control is a big part of growing up. If you are overwhelmed by your feelings or confused about how you really feel, you may try to feel nothing at all—to be numb. Sorting out your true feelings is another basic skill you learn as you mature.

Because everyone else is playing it cool, it may seem as if nobody else feels the way you do. In truth, *everyone* has emotions, whether they express them much or not. These reactions are built into each of us, and are a necessary part of life.

Those who believe that kids don't really get too excited or troubled about anything should listen in on a phone conversation between best friends:

"Did you hear what David said to me? I could have died of shame!"

"Don't you just adore that new boy? He's so cute I could kiss him!"

"If he says that to me once more I'm going to smash his face!"

Sometimes it's easier to share intimate feelings on the phone than face to face. Or you may find yourself confiding in a journal or to your pet. Usually you feel better after talking about your emotions.

The sweeping physical and glandular changes that puberty brings, such as growth spurts, also create extreme emotional changes. Kids complain that they do not know how they are going to feel from one moment to the next—up or down, loving or hostile. Experts call these changes "mood swings" and all kids have them, to one degree or another.

The teen years are a stressful time in other ways, too. All your relationships are changing. You are not quite as close to your parents any more, so you depend more on your friends for support and approval. This brings new worries: "Do my friends think I'm okay or do I act like a jerk sometimes?" "They all are so attractive, I'm afraid I am really ugly!" Some insecurity and shyness is common at this time of life.

The teens also bring the so-called "identity crisis," a time when you find yourself asking basic questions about yourself, your personality, and your future: "Who am I, now that I am almost grown?" "What kind of adult do I want to be?" "What career should I have?" "Who will I marry?" From partying and learning to drive to anticipating the future and falling in love, all these new choices and decisions complicate your once-peaceful life and bring opportunities for all kinds of emotions—fear, insecurity, pride, love, despair, passion, loneliness, envy, and delight.

Love is one emotion that is often misunderstood by younger teenagers. Having a crush on someone may throw a boy or girl into confusion. But this kind of crush is a normal and useful stage in learning to love. Sometimes kids think they have fallen in love forever, when what they are feeling is an infatuation, a surge of physical, even sexual desire that makes people want to be very close. Infatuation—a sudden, intense attraction—is a normal and useful emotion, but not the same as mature, caring, long-term love. Eventually, you will understand the difference.

Insecurity is another emotion that can cause kids a lot of stress and unhappiness. For instance, kids who feel insecure may gang up on somebody, making that person a scapegoat or target for their feelings. To make themselves feel like "insiders" they cause this other person to be the "outsider." Then they can look down on him or her and feel secure—temporarily. This is why there is so much name-calling, rumor-spreading, and forming of cliques in school. It is tough to be the victim, but a little easier when you recognize what's going on.

One giant step towards becoming a happy adult is to learn to express your feelings in ways that work well. For instance, a mature person learns not to pick on other kids when feeling insecure, but to try and figure out what the insecurity stems from and get to work on that. Working to build one's competence is more productive than making someone else unhappy. Kids who are immature tend to hit out when they get mad. Mature kids try to talk things out.

Parents often complain that teenagers are self-centered, but a certain amount of soul searching is inevitable in adolescence. With such a storm of emotion and stress going on, most teenagers feel a real need for times to be private and try to sort it all out. Wise parents make sure they do not fill every minute of a young person's life, but leave room and time for reflection and resolution.

Your feelings about growing up are likely to fluctuate. At times you look forward to maturity, with its new freedoms and opportunities. But at other times you yearn for your love-filled, carefree childhood, and worry about having to take responsibility for your actions as adults must. No wonder your moods switch back and forth when you feel torn this way!

There are big differences in the ways various cultures teach young people to express their emotions. In some countries it is perfectly okay for men to hug each other. Here it is not done very frequently—except when your team has just won a big game, perhaps. In some countries it is okay to yell and wave your arms a lot when you feel happy or sad. Here we are less demonstrative in public.

So you have to figure out ways to express your feelings that not only work for you but fit in with the rest of society, too. However, it rarely works to try to pretend your feelings don't exist. They just sneak around and come out in some unexpected and often unacceptable way. For instance, if your father yells at you in the morning, you may not be able to argue or respond to him. You bury, or suppress, your anger or resentment. Then, in school, you fail your science quiz, even though you studied for it. Or a teacher asks you a question and you answer with a rude, "I don't know and I don't care." You've expressed your anger—but at the wrong time or person.

We live in such a stressful time that learning about yourself is more essential than ever. More decisions have to be made at ever younger ages, as drugs, liquor, and sexuality become issues earlier and earlier. We are bombarded by the media with scary messages about energy, the economy, pollution, and nuclear war. Kids are very disturbed about these worldwide problems. Their concern and anxiety affects their behavior, health, and outlook for the future.

In such a volatile time of life, and in such a turbulent period of history, it is more important than ever to learn to recognize and handle emotions. Understanding your feelings will help you make them work for you, instead of letting them tear you apart. We should all make an effort to try and talk more, and more honestly, about what we feel. When people have real problems about expressing their feelings, they can go to a counselor. Counseling helps a person talk through the buried emotions, take a look at what caused them, and find new ways of expressing them. It helps a person function normally again.

This book will help you get in touch—and stay in touch—with yourself and your feelings. Although we've organized sections in each chapter for girls (about boys) and for boys (about girls), it is important to remember that all of us, male and female, share the same kinds of feelings. So we urge you to read the section for girls about boys even if you are a boy. It might help you gain some insights about yourself, your brother or father or teacher, or others. And, if you are a girl, don't skip the section about girls. You may be surprised to discover the solution to a familiar dilemma, or learn to understand or help a friend, sister, mother, or neighbor.

We hope that with the knowledge you gain from this book you will feel good about yourself and other people, too.

Beth Winship

Disappointment

Dear Beth,

I'm in the seventh grade. My very best friend and I tried out for cheerleading last month. My friend made the squad for the intermediate school teams, and I didn't.

I tried to act happy for her, but inside I felt so terrible. I wanted to cry. I didn't feel right trying to act like I didn't care, because she knows how much I wanted to be a cheerleader. Now we just don't talk about it. But when I go to her house, sometimes she's just getting ready and laying out her cheerleading skirt and top and I feel funny so I just leave. I still want to be friends, but I'm so disappointed, I don't know what to do.

Mandy

■

Dear Mandy,

I know that you must have felt very sad not to make cheerleading. You sound like a very mature girl and a good friend. Disappointments are difficult to accept, but sometimes we need to have experiences that can help us discover what we can do best. This may be a good time to explore other activities. Have you thought about sports you might like to play? Or maybe you can write something for the literary magazine. And, who knows, if in a year you're still interested in cheerleading, you can try out again.

Meanwhile, try not to be too hard on yourself. If you were so sad inside that it was hard to celebrate with your friend, that was a very natural reaction and that feeling will pass. I'm sure she can imagine (almost!) how disappointed you felt. You may have to make an effort to bring the subject up and talk about your feelings with her; this may sound hard but you will feel better. Good friends can discuss everything eventually.

Sometimes, too, it is good if friends have different interests because then they have new and interesting things to share. Some friendships end because of

8

trying to do everything together. You need to be your own individual self.

Beth

■

Dear Beth,

We had this big paper to do for history, and I went all out for an A. I never worked so hard on anything in my life! I read twice as much as we were supposed to and wrote two extra pages. It was neat, too. I was sure I had aced it, but when I got the paper back, all I had was a B−. Teacher said it was good, but there were some errors and some "sloppy thinking."

It's so unfair! I wanted to throw it in his face. I am so disappointed I don't think I'll try any more now.

Bad Mark

■

Dear Bad Mark,

It is very upsetting to work that hard, only to have your expectations disappointed. It is natural to be angry at the one who seemed to let you down. However, you are going to bump into disappointments that seem unfair or unequal over and over again, in different ways, in the future. The way to handle it is first to see if there is something you can do about it. If not, then you have to try and take your lumps and put the episode behind you. Get on with your life without bitterness.

In this case, however, you can do something. Go back to your teacher. Explain, in a rational and respectful way, rather than just complaining, that you worked extra hard on the paper and truly thought you had done a first-class job. Say you would appreciate it if he would go over it with you and explain exactly what was wrong. Perhaps you fell short in organization, or used a poor choice of examples, or didn't express your thoughts very well. This probably will not change your mark, and you will still be disappointed, but you will understand the reasons for it. Then you will not feel so cheated and angry. It will make you more likely to want to make the effort to do better next time.

When you learn something useful, it helps take the sting out of a painful experience.

Beth

You've often heard others, both adults and your friends, use phrases or words that show the extent of their disappointment:

☐ It was a heartbreaker.
☐ It ended on a sour note.
☐ It was like a slap in the face.
☐ I really felt let down.
☐ The whole thing fell through.
☐ It was a bummer.
☐ The bottom fell out.

Disappointments come in all sizes and affect people of all ages. There are so many different kinds of things and happenings that can lead to disappointment. Sometimes it helps to know that others have felt the same way in a similar situation:

"Egg salad!? Mom, you know I wanted peanut butter and jelly!"

"My father said he'd coach our team. He promised— but now he says that there's too much work at the store for him to spend time coaching."

"They've canceled my favorite television program to show the election returns."

"I invited a friend over but she can't come."

"We were supposed to go out, but Mom got sick, so we can't go."

"My parents told me that I could get a new ten-speed bike. Now they've changed their minds and tell me I have to use my brother's old one for at least a year. It's only a three-speed and all of my friends have new ten-speeds."

"I thought my mother was going to be happy because I cleaned my room, but when she came home from work, she didn't even notice."

"My friend Robert was running for president of the

eighth grade and I was his campaign manager. We worked so hard—thinking of new ideas, making posters, writing speeches. He lost the election by just a few votes. There are a lot of kids in my school who think it's just a popularity contest. They really make me mad. I just didn't know who was more disappointed: Robert or me!"

"I really wanted a video hockey game for my birthday and instead my father said, 'Young men your age need watches more than they need another game.' "

"Our seventh-grade class had been planning this dance all spring. Everybody kept telling me that Terry was going to ask me to go with him. I was going to ask this other boy, but I decided to wait until Terry asked me. Guess what? Terry never asked me and someone else asked the other boy. So I went to the dance by myself."

"I'm friends with all these kids at school. I mean, we're always being together, laughing and having fun. I don't understand why, when I'm good friends with all these people, they get asked to parties and I don't get asked. It's a real big school, and my mom says it's because we live so far from each other in other parts of town. Three of the girls I know get to walk to town every day after school, but I have to take the bus home."

Sorting out feelings

You may find it difficult to recognize when friends are disappointed. They may appear to be angry, sad, or distant, or they may be crying. Girls and boys may try to hide how they are feeling. Perhaps they are afraid they would seem silly if they explained how disappointed they felt about something.

When friends are very disappointed, they may be confused about their feelings. There are other emotions that can accompany disappointment, and find-

11

ing the right word to express an emotion is not always easy. Some descriptive words might be:

frustrated	lonely
defeated	angry
overwhelmed	feeling used
disillusioned	victimized
sad	hurt
lost	powerless
dissatisfied	

There are more similarities than differences when it comes to girls and boys and disappointment. When a boy is very disappointed, he feels just as confused as a girl, but he may behave differently. A boy may have learned to hide disappointment behind another emotion. He may act angry or act as if he does not care. He may feel like crying and he really should; crying is a very positive way of releasing feelings. But he may have learned (from family, friends, television) that he should control his crying, be tough, "act like a man." Covering his disappointment, he may react physically—playing a fierce game of basketball or running a mile. Or sometimes a friend may joke about something that happened, when inside he or she is really very disappointed.

Do others feel the way I feel?

Psychiatrists, psychologists, and sociologists are people who study emotions, feelings, and ways people behave. They study not only abnormal behaviors, but also normal behaviors.

You may wonder sometimes if the way you feel is similar to how others feel. One study asked girls and boys thirteen to eighteen years old to think about their feelings. One statement/question they were asked had to do with having hurt feelings, an experience related to disappointment.

This study of about 500 girls and boys showed the following:

☐ More teenage girls report their feelings are easily hurt than boys.
☐ Younger teenage boys' feelings are more easily hurt than older boys'.
☐ Younger teenage girls' feelings are slightly less easily hurt than older teenage girls'.

According to the study, boys report their feelings are less easily hurt as they get older; girls report that their feelings are more easily hurt as they get older. It is possible that boys were hiding their real feelings. Or perhaps boys have been brought up to endure more stress and they have become more used to accepting criticism. Girls may have been more protected when they were little; their parents may have comforted them more when their feelings were hurt. So their feelings are more easily hurt as teenagers.

Competition and failure

We live in a very competitive world. Each of us competes for something at one time or another—whether we choose to compete or not. In school, you may compete:

☐ for a class election
☐ for a team
☐ for a high academic position in the class
☐ for a part in a school play
☐ for a place in the lunch line

At home, you may compete:

☐ for a parent's attention
☐ for your favorite seat at the table
☐ for your choice of television program
☐ for the last piece of pie

And with friends, you may compete to be:

- ☐ the best dressed
- ☐ the fastest runner
- ☐ the most popular
- ☐ the funniest
- ☐ a member or a leader in a particular clique or group

Some individuals are very competitive, some are slightly competitive, and some are not competitive at all. Our feelings about competition come from:

- ☐ our basic personality (introverted, shy; extroverted, outgoing)
- ☐ our early family experiences
- ☐ our early school experiences
- ☐ our early experiences in our neighborhood

The way we handle or react to competition is also a product of these combined experiences. Some people seek competition, while others avoid it—but all of us compete one way or another. And competing, of course, means succeeding or failing.

You may wonder why some people seem to handle failure better than others. For instance, you may have

friends who try out for something and, even if they fail, are always willing to try again.

The person who does not give up—who is not devastated for life by this single experience—may be a person who can learn from his or her failure. Failing a math test does not mean you are a terrible math student; failing a swimming test does not mean you are hopeless at swimming forever. It is helpful to be honest with yourself, to examine what has happened and to try to improve in that area. Of course, you should also set realistic goals; you are not ready for the Olympic ski team if you have barely started skiing!

Coping with disappointment

What can a person do to deal with disappointment? Well, you could yell, cry, go running or bike riding, or write to a newspaper columnist for advice.

One girl said she just goes into her room by herself. Another said she feels lucky because she can talk to her dog. Her advice for when you are feeling disappointed: "Talk to pets—they listen!"

Other girls said:

"I just want people to forget it!"

"I hate those 'pity' looks, especially from mothers. They can make it the hardest."

"Disappointment is a private thing; I just want to be alone."

"I just want life to go on—quickly!"

"It's lousy when nobody notices you're disappointed. Sometimes I used to act like a real brat until somebody would finally say, 'What's wrong with you?' "

Boys commented:

"I don't want people to remember it!"

"My mother gives me this real sorrowful look. Who needs that? If only she knew she was making it worse."

15

"I wish they'd leave me alone when I feel disappointed."

"I know life goes on, but why can't it go much faster just this one time?"

"I like it when my parents help me through bad times. I know they really love me."

Even though girls and boys may become disappointed over slightly different things and although they may handle disappointment a little differently, they basically experience the same feeling.

Others can help

Asking a grandparent, father, mother, or older sister or brother to tell you about their disappointments is sometimes helpful. Little disappointments, which

seemed big at the time, are often remembered throughout life. And sometimes disappointments that seem catastrophic at the time are forgotten.

When a friend you care about seems disappointed, try to figure out why he or she is feeling that way. This may be hard, even with a person you have known for a long time. Try to see if there are any other emotions mixed with the disappointment.

Here are a few suggestions on how to show friends that you understand their feelings of disappointment:

1. You might think of something fun to do to take their mind off their problems for a little while.
2. You might share a similar experience you have had. But be careful about this—when people are feeling down, they sometimes can't believe that anybody else has ever felt as down as they do.
3. If it is a problem that can be solved, maybe you could help them decide what to do.
4. You might make a card or write a note.
5. You might let them have a little time alone.

If you cannot figure out what has caused the disappointment, just letting your friend know that you care may help. The best thing you can do as a friend is try to understand. Let your friend know that you understand and that you would like to listen if talking would help.

Worry

Dear Beth,

My grandmother had a heart attack and was in intensive care. She's better now, but it started me worrying. I just realized that she is going to die sometime—maybe soon. I hate to think about it. And my parents will die, too. What would become of me?

Orphan?

Dear Orphan,

The discovery that every single person is mortal hits most people sometime during their teens with an abrupt jolt. You knew about death before, of course, but never fully realized its significance. Behind this concern lies one of all children's most basic worries—that of being abandoned. But realistically, most parents live to play with their own grandchildren. By that time you will be a fully independent adult, capable of looking after yourself and others as well.

Parents do sometimes die earlier, but their children *are* usually looked after. Other relatives or friends love them and bring them up. If no one is able to do this, there are agencies who care for such children.

Underneath these other concerns, you may also be worried about dying yourself. Death is scary, because nobody knows what really happens after they die. Deeply religious people believe in life after death. Others think it is just a long, long sleep. But one thing is certain: death is part of life. Every single thing that lives must die. However, the memory of you lingers on in the hearts of those who loved you. If you have children, something of you continues in the genetic heritage you pass along. As you grow up, you gradually adjust to the idea by learning to think about life instead of worrying about death.

Beth

Dear Beth,

I'm going to high school this fall, and I'm kind of concerned about a couple of things. It's a big regional school, with over four thousand kids, and I'll only know about ten of them. Also, I'm kind of small for my age. Some of my friends call me "Shrimp" but they're only kidding. In high school I hear big guys kick you around, and even beat people up. What can I do?

Paul the Shrimp

■

Dear Paul,

The stories are probably exaggerated. While there are incidents of violence in some schools today, people like to make things sound worse than they are.

Remember, everyone in the huge freshman class will also be new: they will not know their way around any better than you do. Many schools have freshman orientation, to help you learn your way around.

It helps if you can develop a plan of action. Hang onto your old friends at first. There is safety in numbers, for one thing, and you can all use the moral support until you make new friends. Go out for activities that give you an instant group of new friends, such as a sports team, the band, or shop. You'll be doing something you enjoy and meeting other kids.

As for your height, you will grow eventually, although it may take you a little longer than your friends. Meanwhile, learn how to cope with name-calling or teasing with a friendly or humorous quip. Even bullies find it hard to pick on a guy who makes them laugh.

Beth

■

Dear Beth,

I have this friend and he and his sister are twins. The only thing is that he is really worried because she is about four inches taller than he is. He told me that his father said that he'd catch up. I think his father just told him that to make him feel okay and not worry, but it still bothers him. The other guys in the sixth grade pick on my friend because his sister is taller. What can you tell me about this? Is his father telling the truth?

Worrywart

If you were to look up the word *worry* in the diction-
ary, you would find that the meaning that best fits the
concerns of these letter writers is: a troubled state of
mind, anxiety, distress, care, uneasiness.

Everyone worries—babies, kids, teenagers, grownups. When people are worried, they look serious, puz-
zled. They appear tense and anxious; they may frown
a lot or wrinkle their eyebrows. They may seem distant. ("You look like you're a million miles away.") Or
you may think that they are listening to you and gradually realize that they aren't.

As with other feelings and emotions, there are big
worries and little ones. Big worries are considered to
be serious, while little worries are regarded as less important . . . except when you are the one who is
worried.

Smaller worries are more transient. They are dilemmas that arise now and then rather than persisting
day after day, or things that we get over soon. Little
worries might be:

□ What if I miss my bus?
□ Should I eat the last piece of cake?
□ Will my friends be mad at me if I don't want to go to
the game?
□ I hope I pass my English test.
□ What if our team loses another game?

Big worries might be:

□ How will my parents react to my report card? I failed
math.
□ Will my mother and father ever get back together
again?
□ Will my grandmother be all right? She lives alone
and hasn't been feeling well.
□ What would happen if I got stoned or drunk?
□ Will my father be all right after his operation?

□ What will happen if they open the nuclear power plant near our town?

□ Will I ever be the right size?

□ Do you suppose this car could crash?

□ If a boy is usually nice, will he be different when he's stoned?

□ Will my parents ever leave me alone?

Notice that many of the big worries concern the health or well-being of someone else. People often feel most troubled when they are worried about things they cannot change—another's health, their parents' decisions, their own height.

Worrywart's concern

There are many worries related to physical growth and development. Girls worry about weight, height, breast size, and body shape. Boys worry about height, weight, penis size, and body shape or physique.

Worrywart's friend has a problem because his twelve-year-old twin sister is taller and bigger than he is. This is usually normal; the average twelve-year-old girl is taller and heavier than the average boy of the same age. Below is a height and weight table that may answer some questions:

Sex	Age	Average Height (inches)	Average Weight (pounds)
girl	12	59.6	91.4
boy	12	58.9	87.5

However, the tendency for girls to be taller and heavier than boys is true only up until around fourteen years of age. Then, boys usually become heavier and taller. The following table shows the changes from ages thirteen through sixteen:

21

Sex	Age	Average Height (inches)	Average Weight (pounds)
girl	13	61.9	101.4
boy	13	61.6	98.9
girl	14	63.1	110.6
boy	14	64.2	111.7
girl	15	63.7	118.1
boy	15	66.2	123.6
girl	16	63.9	123.0
boy	16	68.3	130.6

So Worrywart can tell his friend that his father's advice was good and that things will probably change.

Psychosomatic illnesses

You may have heard people express their feelings of worry with phrases like:

"You worry me to death."
"I worried my head off all night."
"I was so worried I could have killed you."
"You worry me sick."

Of course these are exaggerations. No one would kill someone just because he made them worry. And of course someone's head would not drop off from worrying. However, you can become sick from worrying.

A *psychosomatic* illness is one that begins in the mind, or psyche, when someone is under stress. Some emotions that cause stress are worry, anger, loneliness, sadness, passion, and excitement. If life stresses become too much, the psychosomatic illness changes from an emotional pain into a physical pain or condition. Examples of these illnesses are severe or migraine headaches, asthma, and ulcers. Psychosomatic illnesses are not consciously caused by us, nor can we always recognize how stress is contributing to or aggravating a physical condition. Sometimes the illness begins with the sudden presence of a severe physical pain, or it develops gradually.

Case Study

Annie is thirteen years old and lives with her recently divorced mother. Annie misses her father very much and does not understand why her parents are divorced; no one has really explained it to her. Annie's mother is thirty-three years old. She not only has to take care of Annie; she must also work, pay the bills, and lead her own life. Lately, Annie's mother has been moody and irritable because of the worry and stress in her life. So every time Annie does something wrong, her mother screams at her. Sometimes Annie appears to anger her mother for no particular reason. Annie starts to worry every time her mother screams a lot. Suddenly Annie begins complaining of bad headaches. She even misses school because of them. Her mother takes her to a doctor to find out what's causing the headaches. The doctor tells them that there is no physical reason for them and gives Annie and her mother the name of a psychologist.

After two appointments with Annie, the psychologist finds out what is causing the headaches: Annie's confusion about and inability to respond directly to her mother's yelling. The psychologist then meets with Annie and her mother a few times to help them understand the cause of Annie's pain. Together they look for new ways for the mother to deal with Annie's behavior and for Annie to cope with her mother's moods.

The more Annie learned about her mother and herself, the less she worried, and the easier it was for her to talk about her confusion. After a few more visits, Annie's mother reported that Annie's headaches were beginning to occur less often.

▬▬▬

The encouraging ending of this case study is due to the assistance of an outside helper—in this instance, a psychologist. When severe worries or anxieties get out of control and don't go away over time (whether or not they result in psychosomatic symptoms like Annie's headaches), it is vital to find someone to help. Annie and her mother talked to a doctor, and then a psychologist. Sometimes a caring friend or an adult you trust will be all you need. At other times, a professional will be most helpful. Doctors, school guidance counselors or social workers, ministers, and many service and counseling agencies are there to help you get over any kind of serious, chronic worry or unhappiness. For suggestions on how to find the right helper for you, see page 163.

Worrying: a play in one act

PETE I was kind of scared when my dog was having puppies. Everyone kept saying, "Oh, don't worry. It's natural. Dogs know what to do." Fine—but what was I supposed to do?

CARMEN Mothers. Mothers worry about the silliest things. Sometimes I get mad at my mother when she tells me about things I never even thought of.

JOSH Yeah, like worrying about being kidnapped or having an accident or getting lost. I have enough worries without someone adding more!

DEBBIE Well, I really do worry when it's dark and I'm walking alone. Even when I'm with a friend, I worry about being raped or mugged.

PETE You need a self-defense course. Then you won't worry so much!

CARMEN Seriously, though. You shouldn't walk home alone.

JOSH When I'm worried, I try to figure out what I can do to feel less worried—like before a test. If I've studied I try to relax and think positively. It works—usually.

DEBBIE And if I'm worried about a friend, I call her up as soon as I can and tell her how I'm feeling. I always feel better when I let her know how I feel.

How to stop worrying

If you find that you are very worried you may need some time to unwind before you can tackle your problems. Here are some simple things you can do to relax:

- ☐ Take a solitary bike ride.
- ☐ Take a walk in the woods.
- ☐ Use some time alone in your room just thinking or crying.
- ☐ Listen to music.
- ☐ Check your library for books or tapes that teach relaxation techniques.

The basic idea of a relaxation exercise is to get each part of your body to release its tension gradually. You do this by sending messages to relax each body part: muscles, limbs, joints, organs. Even a brief five- or

ten-minute relaxation session may clear your mind and help you cope better.

Begin by lying on your back on the floor. Close your eyes and take a few deep breaths. Slowly and silently instruct each body part to relax. Begin with your toes, then your feet, ankles, calves, thighs, and so on. The shoulders, neck, and face tend to hold a lot of tension, so it's important to remember to relax them. Imagine the tension leaving your body with every breath you take. Relax your jaw muscles, cheeks, eyes, forehead. When your body is completely relaxed (it may feel kind of heavy), lie quietly and breathe slowly and deeply. Try to picture a tranquil scene such as gentle waves on a beach, warm sand between your toes, a beautiful sunset, or the twinkling of city lights at dusk. Contemplate this scene for a while, then return your concentration to the room you're in and open your eyes. Chances are you'll feel refreshed . . . and a little less anxious.

Embarrassment

Dear Beth,

My mom is really a great mother most of the time, but sometimes she drinks too much, and then she yells and screams at people for no reason. Once I brought friends home from school and found her passed out on the couch. I was so embarrassed I could have died! I told them Mom worked late and had to sleep but I don't know if they believed me.

Now I keep making up excuses why I won't ask them over. I walk around with this big guilty secret inside me, and would die of shame if I thought kids were saying "Her mother drinks."

Mortified

■

Dear Mortified,

It is a constant burden worrying that a parent may drink too much, lose control, and disgrace the family. We all take pride in our families and feel ashamed when one member behaves badly. You need to realize, first of all, that you are not responsible for your mother's drinking. In addition, alcoholism is not uncommon; it is almost certain that others in your class have this same problem in their family and are keeping it a secret too.

While you naturally want to avoid embarrassing situations such as the one you had, your good friends would not judge you if it happened again. They know your mother's behavior is not your fault.

You can do something to help yourself, however, by joining an Alateen group. Alateen is a self-help group of teenagers, each of whom has an alcoholic parent. In the group, kids learn what the disease is about and how to live without feeling ashamed. They also learn that they can still love that parent; and that they are neither the cause of their parent's drinking problem nor responsible for curing it. Alateen helps kids cope and stay healthy themselves. Look for your local group in the phone book under Alateen or Al-Anon, or under Alcoholics Anonymous if neither of the other names is listed.

Beth

■

Dear Beth,

In my school a boy can take home economics. I thought it would be fun, so I took it. Our last project was making aprons. I made one for my mother. Last Monday when I came to school a lot of the guys were laughing at me and I didn't know why. I found out when I looked in the display case used by my home economics teacher. In the case were ten aprons. Nine belonged to girls and the tenth one was mine! I can't tell you how embarrassed I was. I heard one of the guys say (loud enough for everyone to hear), "Nice apron Andy made. I think I'll ask him to make one for my mommy." Everyone cracked up and I felt about an inch tall. Even my best friend laughed. What can I do now to prove that I'm not a sissy?

Andy

■

Dear Andy,

It is always embarrassing to be singled out, but you are to be admired. You chose to take home economics because you were interested in the course. You were willing to risk being the only boy in an all-girl class because you thought the subject was of interest to you. And, in fact, it turned out that you enjoyed the class.

It may help to remember that in a few days the boys who laughed will have forgotten all about it. Maybe they made a big issue of it because they didn't have the courage to take home economics, even though it sounded like fun to them too.

Maybe years from now, you can tell this story and laugh!

Beth

Embarrassment is a feeling that can be caused by a general, long-lasting situation (Mortified's letter about her mother), or by a specific brief or unexpected moment or experience (Andy's letter about the apron).

When embarrassment is related to a general, long-lasting situation, the feeling is probably mixed with feelings of worry, helplessness, sadness, and anger. Learning to cope with all these feelings will take time. Also, learning to live with the situation will require a concentrated effort. You must sort out the emotions and understand the facts. Then you can develop strategies and solutions.

It is important in these situations to separate shame from embarrassment. Along with both feelings comes a sensation of being uncomfortable and self-conscious. Shame often includes a feeling of disgrace or dishonor. There can also be a feeling of guilt. Mortified felt both ashamed and embarrassed. She felt disgraced by her mother's behavior and guilty because she felt somehow responsible for her mom's behavior. In Andy's case, he was only embarrassed. Another factor in sorting out shame and embarrassment is whether or not you are in control of the situation. For example, Andy might choose not to continue taking home economics—that is in his control. On the other hand, Mortified cannot control her mother's behavior. She is faced with a more difficult problem.

Some embarrassing moments are painful

Some experiences (like Mortified's) are too embarrassing, too devastating ever to laugh about. Often these feelings and memories are connected with more lasting, enduring situations—situations like being too tall or too short, or being very shy. Other painful experiences include being the object of a cruel hoax or joke; or boasting that you could do something (like water-skiing) and then failing; or problems at home.

Some feelings and hurtful memories are related to long-lasting experiences with our families. Mortified describes one of the troubling aspects of living with an alcoholic parent. Another source of pain may be an older brother or sister, ahead of you in school, who is always getting into trouble. It is embarrassing when everyone knows that you are related to him or her and you have the same name. (It can also be hard to live up to the successful reputation of an older brother or sister; teachers may assume you are going to follow in the footsteps of the higher achiever and may constantly compare you to him or her.) Frequently, you may have to contend with an embarrassing scene at home, such as when your parents are fighting and a friend is over, or when you are scolded in front of a friend.

In these situations, unlike lighter (and funnier) embarrassments, you are both ashamed and embarrassed by the behavior of someone you cannot control. Feeling out of control can make you sad, or angry, or resentful.

The sad embarrassments are the hardest to get over. You feel like you want to escape—flee, run away, change your name. People do all of these; but in the end nothing changes, because the hurt and embarrassment are locked in your memory. For Mortified, the sight of her mother drunk and passed out on the couch in front of her friends is now a permanent memory. As we mature, we learn to handle difficult experiences like Mortified's. She must discover that she is not to blame for her mother's problems, that no one will accuse her of causing them. However, it is very unlikely that Mortified is going to be able to cope with her mother's problem by herself. She needs to seek out a helping person or group that can assist her. Eventually, talking and working through her feelings, as well as the passage of time, will help heal the pain of Mortified's situation.

Here are some words and phrases that describe embarrassment:

"I was *humiliated*."
"I wanted to *dig a hole and climb in it*."
"I felt so *isolated*."
"I *turned as red as a beet*."
"I was *chagrined*."
"I could have *died!*"

My most embarrassing moment . . .

Embarrassment often comes in brief moments and experiences—moments that are a complete surprise, that you cannot anticipate or expect.

"Once I was sitting in a booth with some girls. One of the girls got mad because some boys were fooling with the juke box and the song she had paid for and wanted to hear didn't play. All of a sudden, she screamed across the room at them and everyone—well, all the boys—stared at us. I was so embarrassed."

"When my father talks to my friends, and he thinks he's funny and he goes on and on—I get embarrassed."

"I'm embarrassed when my mother swears in front of my friends."

"What's embarrassing is when you really like someone, and then right when you're standing there, a friend says real loud to that person that you like him or her. I had that happen and it was awful. I don't know why kids do that."

"I hate it when everyone's standing around and somebody tells you that someone really likes you. And then you realize that the person who told you was only joking, just fooling around."

"It's embarrassing when your gym teacher asks you to demonstrate something for the class."

"I get so embarrassed when my math teacher calls me a nickname (like Tiger!), especially if I don't know the answer and didn't come for special help like I was supposed to and he makes a big deal out of it."

"One time the teacher sent me to find a tape in the cabinet. I didn't know which cabinet she meant, and I was searching everywhere for it! I felt so stupid."

"It's embarrassing when you invite someone over to your house . . . and then you don't feel good and you wish they'd go home. Or when you're at someone's house and you get sick. Once I threw up at my friend's house. I felt so dumb!"

What does embarrassment feel like? When you are embarrassed you may feel:

dizzy	as if you cannot see
like disappearing	red in the face (blushing)
like killing the person who embarrassed you	hot or flushed
like a jerk	

Do boys and girls get embarrassed over different things?

Of course. There are some things that only girls get embarrassed over, and some things that only boys find embarrassing.

Girls

Girls are embarrassed (and angry!) when boys or girls use words to describe them that refer to their bodies, like "flatso" or "stacked." Girls may be embarrassed when they are menstruating and have to ask a teacher to excuse them from class to go to the nurse or the bathroom (especially getting that very first menstrual period at school). Girls may be embarrassed if they don't know whether to offer to pay their share on a date.

Boys

Boys may be embarrassed if they are shorter or weaker than other boys their own age. Boys may be more embarrassed than girls to show their emotions in front of friends, especially if they are afraid or sad.

Puberty can cause some very embarrassing moments for boys. One of the first things to signal the beginning of puberty is a wet dream (nocturnal emission). This is an unintended discharge of semen from a boy's penis as he sleeps. He may be embarrassed that other family members might discover the wet sheets or pyjamas, or that he has sexual feelings that aren't controlled. Or a boy may, for no reason whatsoever, get an erection. This could happen during his math class, in the lunch line, or while doing his homework. You will notice that none of these situations has anything to do with sex. The erection is caused by hormones and is completely unintentional. You can imagine how embarrassing this can be if someone else notices.

Another physical change that can be disturbing occurs when a boy's voice changes. During puberty, boys' vocal cords are thickening. This process brings about the older male's husky voice and creates a man's Adam's apple. Of course it doesn't happen overnight; it takes a while. However, while it is changing, a boy's voice can be very undependable. Imagine that you are asking a girl out for the first time. Then, right in the middle of your invitation, your voice cracks and you sound like a kid (or a girl). What do you do? You probably break out in a sweat!

It can be embarrassing for a boy to take a group shower. Girls usually have the option of either a private stall or a group shower, but boys often don't have a choice. In the group shower there is no place for privacy. If someone is unsure of his body—he thinks he has a little too much baby fat, or he worries that his penis is smaller than those of the other guys, or he has little or no pubic hair yet—a group shower can be an event he dreads.

Some embarrassing moments are funny

Some embarrassing moments you can laugh about later with your friends.

"Remember the time I didn't have enough money when I got to the cash register?"

"Remember when John told that stupid joke, and everyone else was laughing but I didn't get it?"

"Remember how nervous I was, and I didn't want to

go to school when I had my hair cut . . . and my mother made me go?"

"Remember the year we both wore those weird T-shirts all the time, every day, everywhere we went? I wonder what people thought."

"Remember when I bumped right into Mr. D.—that cute teacher we had a crush on?"

"Remember when I dropped my lunch tray and the Jello went all over the floor?"

"Remember when I pronounced Tucson 'Tuk-son'?"

"Remember when I broke that fancy glass at Joe's house?"

Recovering from and covering up embarrassment

A sense of humor helps! Living through an embarrassing moment or experience can be hard. It helps to realize that somebody, somewhere, sometime, has had the same experience (or worse!).

☐ It helps to be able to laugh at yourself, either alone or with others.

☐ It helps to tell a friend about it and see if he or she has had anything similar happen.

Why do kids laugh when someone is embarrassed?

Laughing can be a nervous reaction. The kids who are watching an embarrassing incident (someone tripping over a shoelace or being scolded by a teacher or parent) know that what has happened to the other person could easily have happened to them. They find it unbearable to imagine how they would feel in the same predicament, so their laughter may be a nervous cover-up for their own fear of having the same thing happen to them.

Why do some boys (and girls) act tough when they are embarrassed?

Some kids react to embarrassment by trying to cover it up with put-downs like "It's going to be a stupid team anyway; I'm glad I didn't make it." Some kids learn early that the best defense is a good offense: protect your self-image even if you have to make someone else look bad. Many people also learn the art of rationalization. They may blame someone else for what they may see as an embarrassing situation: "I'm too good for them" or "The drama club didn't give me a fair chance."

They may also cover their embarrassment or hurt by acting out angry behaviors. For instance, because they were embarrassed in the classroom by a teacher during the day, they might break a window after school, or vandalize a car or building; or they may find somebody else to humiliate and embarrass, to pick on or harass, thinking that they can make somebody else feel as bad or worse than they did. These cover-ups rarely work. People who have been embarrassed and react by doing these things do not feel any better; in fact, they'll probably feel worse.

How can you help a friend who feels embarrassed?

Verbally:

☐ You can assure the person that you are still his or her friend.
☐ You can share an experience of your own.
☐ You can search for the right words to help your friend express a particular feeling: *ashamed, humiliated, devastated, frustrated, mortified, isolated.*

Nonverbally, the right look or gesture of understanding can help: a quick hug or a pat on the shoulder may be just what a person needs to get through the moment.

Why can you feel embarrassed when something good is happening?

When you have just won a race, or are receiving an award, or being complimented, you may feel embarrassed. You may be smiling or crying or not know what to say. Being the center of attention feels good, but it can also be embarrassing! But people enjoy celebrating with each other, so try to relax and simply enjoy the good feeling.

Love, Love, Love

There are many kinds of love. We love others and, in a sense, we love ourselves. We use the word *love* in so many different ways that it is difficult to define. The way you love your parents is different from the way you love your sisters and brothers. The romantic love you feel in an intimate friendship is different from the love you have for other friends. The word *love* expresses a variety of feelings, grand and small: "I love the beach"; "I love rock music"; "I love tennis."

There are similarities and differences in how girls and boys experience love. Because it is such a complex subject, this chapter is divided into three parts which cover the many aspects of love:

I. *How Do I Love You?*
—a general discussion about some kinds of love and the similarities among relationships with family and friends, young and old, male and female.

II. *For Girls About Boys*
—a look at boys' friendships with girls and boys.

III. *For Boys About Girls*
—ten love dilemmas; how to fall in (and out) of love.

I. How Do I Love You?

You may experience love in many ways: as a warm, protected feeling; through sharing and mutual caring; as a desire to laugh and enjoy being with each other; as a time to be sad or worried together. Love can be joyous and happy or painful and frightening. Love can be lonely, and love can be full of wonderful surprises.

You may find love:

☐ With older friends, younger friends, peers.
☐ With friends of the same or opposite sex.
☐ With parents and guardians and grandparents.
☐ With sisters, brothers, cousins.
☐ With pets or other animals.
☐ Through a chance encounter with a person you have never met before, or from a distance.
☐ Alone, imagining a wonderful moment of happiness or joy.
☐ As you enjoy a film, poem, or book and share another's experience.

All in the family

"My mother drives me nuts! I can't stand my little brother! I hate this house and everybody and everything in it!"

Can this be love? Yes it can. Within a family there is a love that can withstand ups and downs, occasionally unreasonable outbursts, periods of good communication, and times when communication is difficult or impossible. The freedom to think out loud, to express your feelings and thoughts openly, to be able to let it all out generally happens within that environment of caring and loving usually known as "family." Naturally, there is a limit to this kind of venting. You may have friends who can speak their minds at home and other friends who would not dare. But the irritations and frustrations you feel from living closely with your family generally are fleeting. The love shared by a family can run very deep, despite conflicts and problems.

Love within a family is demonstrated every day: by parents working to support and care for children, by children assuming household responsibilities, by family members responding to each other's needs—listening, giving, advising. And, though family love can be very strong, kids must not assume that it doesn't require some effort. A parent may demand that you do certain things (homework, chores, caring for siblings); a parent, in turn, must give back to you the guidance and support you need for love to flourish within your family.

This unstated love, often called *unconditional love* (that which doesn't have any conditions or requirements) is demonstrated when somebody outside the family criticizes a parent or sibling. You may be very angry at your brother, but if someone else puts him down, your loyalty will surface and you will not allow that person to ridicule him. Although you may not always admit to your sister how proud you are of her, inside you maintain a closeness to her and a sense of pride in her accomplishments, as she does in yours.

You may be most aware of unconditional love when you are troubled or in need. Even though you and your parents may disagree about some things, you may find that you often turn to each other for advice, comfort, or support. You may need help handling a school conflict, or coping with a tragedy that has occurred to a friend. Or a parent may be sad or depressed and need and respond to the love you offer. These interactions are expressions of love.

Your family may be different from your friends' families. You might have a mother, a stepfather, one brother, and one sister. One friend might have a mother and two brothers. Someone else might have a grandfather and an uncle who live with his or her parents and siblings. The important thing about a family is not who is in it, but the closeness and attachment you feel for one another.

Helping a friend experience love

Sometimes families are under stress, and individuals within the family may be unable to sense or respond to each other's needs. If you have a friend who is having problems within or outside the family, you can help:

☐ Surprise her by preparing a picnic lunch on a snowy afternoon.
☐ Plan a surprise party for his birthday.
☐ Send her a friendship card or a letter on a special occasion.
☐ Invite him to hike to an especially beautiful spot you've discovered—a meadow, marsh, or stream.
☐ Ask to borrow her bike and spend the afternoon oiling, cleaning, tuning, and polishing it for her.
☐ Pick a bouquet of spring wild flowers and put them in his house anonymously.
☐ Invite her to see a movie that you especially enjoyed.
☐ If you have a favorite writer, introduce your friend to that author's books.

Furry, feathered, and other friends

A playful puppy, newborn kittens, a familiar bark as you enter the house—pets and animals have an important place in the lives of many people. Attachments to animals can be strong. Loving and caring for your cat or dog can provide hours of fun, companionship, and work. Having a pet also brings responsibilities and worried times. If your pet is lost, sick, hurt, or growing old, the concern you feel is as significant as your feelings for people. Emotions connected with pets can be quite like those you experience with friends and family—jealousy, helplessness, anger, worry. If you own a pony or horse, for instance, you may rely on each other to train and perform; whether for pleasure or competition, you count and depend on each other. This requires commitment, consistent caring, and love.

You most likely developed your fondness for a particular kind of pet by observing the attitudes of one or both of your parents: you will have this sensitivity and knowledge about animals throughout your life. You will reexperience the good feelings with future pets and when you are living away from home.

Sometimes when a family has a pet, the pet is especially close to one family member, possibly the person who feeds it or cares for it the most, or perhaps the person who talks to it the most. This can create feelings between family members that may be difficult. Perhaps you can work out an arrangement that equalizes the pet's relationships with different members of its family. You could take turns caring for it, or make sure each person gets to play with the pet for a certain amount of time each week. Sometimes, however, it isn't possible to change patterns that have already been set and you just might have to accept the situation.

A novel kind of love

Another way people experience love and the many emotions connected to it is through reading. You have probably read a book that had meaning for your life, a book that allowed you to share another's experience, see how they solved problems, and understand how they developed as people, coped with difficulties, or fell in love.

Through reading you can explore your own emotions. You can imagine how it might feel to compete and fail, to compete and win, to overcome a physical handicap, or to endure a family crisis or natural disaster. You can experience separation, mourning and loss, pride, joy, and love. You may even begin to fantasize about the kind of person you could fall in love with in real life, or the qualities that are important to you in people who inspire admiration or adoration. Through your imagination you can learn about and prepare for real-life situations.

Reading can introduce you to heroes and mentors, too. Almost everybody has met at some point (in real life or through reading) a person they would like to be like, or someone who has taught or guided them. You will be most fortunate in a lifetime to have two or three experiences with an important role model or teacher. This person may be:

☐ a grandparent who taught you special secrets
☐ a teacher through whom you discovered a new interest or who helped you define your goals
☐ a poet who helped you "see" and "listen" in new ways
☐ a neighbor or family friend whom you are comfortable talking or being with

If you have not met someone special like this—start looking!

II. For Girls about Boys

Dear Beth,

I think I like this girl in my class a lot. She is in my seventh-grade Spanish class. The trouble is that none of the guys I hang around with like girls. They think girls are goofy and do stupid things. In my Spanish class the teacher makes kids talk to each other in Spanish. The other day he told me and her to talk to each other about the weather in front of the class. He also told us to look at each other when we talked. I turned red; some of the guys laughed and she giggled. I wanted to disappear. After class she said it was nice and so was I. The guys keep making fun of me and won't let it die. They even made up a poem about us.

Twelve and Don't Know What to Do

■

Dear Don't Know What to Do,

You are not alone. You are starting to enter a period of your life when sexual feelings are coming alive. In the beginning, boys feel unsure, just as you do. In your case it is even more difficult because you think you are perhaps the first one of your group to get these feelings. Some of the other guys may be having the same feelings. They too may not know what to make of them or what to do about them.

There is a period of time in boys' lives when they want nothing at all to do with girls. They call girls names like "goofy," "stupid," and "dumb," or any thing else that shows contempt or disdain. But then comes a time, only a year or two later, when a boy can't wait to have a girl friend. Girls are no longer merely pals or part of the gang. They take on a new status; they become important for a new reason, not because they're fun to pay with, but because boy-girl relationships signal growth and maturity. In the beginning of this stage of life, boys don't know how to act; they are unsure of what to do. They may try asking an older brother, reading books, or saying something like this to their fathers: "I have this friend, see, and he doesn't know what to do when he's with this girl. . . ." Even when a boy learns from others that what he feels is normal, he may fumble and act silly when he is actually with girls. The early period of not knowing what to do with girls— of embarrassment, shyness, feeling flushed and sweaty when you are around a girl—is a healthy part of growing. The feelings of awkwardness will pass as you get older and feel more comfortable in front of girls.

You are probably wondering if she feels the same way you do. No one can tell you for sure. However, one sign of how she feels is that she said you were nice. She also said she enjoyed talking with you in class. These are good clues, but only you can decide what to do next.

As far as the poems go, you will find that even older boys do things like this. They enjoy kidding each other about the opposite sex. You'll have to learn to live with it.

Beth

■

It is important to remember that during early adolescence (around the ages of eleven to fourteen years) boys tend to develop slower than girls, physically, socially, and emotionally. They may not be interested in forming relationships with girls yet; often they would rather hang around with the guys. However, as these boys become teenagers, they catch up socially and emotionally with girls their age. Physically, in most cases, boys then overtake the girls; they become stronger and taller (see height and weight tables in the chapter on worry).

In this chapter the discussion will center on the first awakening of boys' feelings about girls. You will recognize some situations that boys may find themselves in before they are fully ready to relate to girls comfortably. It's all part of maturing and learning about each other.

Infatuation

During puberty, hormones are produced which cause complex physical changes in boys—voice changes, hair growth (pubic, underarm, chest, facial), increased height, and semen production. These hormones account for sexual energy and feelings that seem new, strange, and often scary or confusing. Fantasies and daydreaming are healthy ways for a boy to release this new kind of energy. In his mind he can experiment with behaviors that will go with the physical and emotional changes as he matures.

The first sign of feelings for the opposite sex in boys often comes in the form of infatuation, a feeling of attraction that can be confused with love. An infatuation (also called a "crush" or "puppy love") is an intense feeling for someone, usually someone older. It could be the boy's teacher, a next-door neighbor, the cashier at the supermarket, or a music or film star. The boy usually keeps these feelings secret and does not share them with anyone, even his best friend. Infatuations usually fade away in time, whereas love—true love—endures.

When girls become infatuated with someone, they

think a lot about situations that are romantic, like getting married and having a family. Boys going through this phase, however, think about heroic acts they might perform that would capture a girl's attention. Some examples of boys' typical infatuation fantasies are:

☐ He saves his teacher from a burning building. His heroism causes her to fall in love with him.
☐ Stopping a robbery at the store causes the pretty cashier to fall in love with him because she thinks he is very brave and strong.
☐ A famous woman rock singer notices his fantastic guitar playing and he becomes her constant companion.

In these fantasies or daydreams, the boy is a hero who wins the heart of a woman. Through fantasy, a boy can imagine himself as strong and confident. He can explore his feelings without risking embarrassment or failure as he might in real life.

A boy may also have crushes on girls his own age or only slightly older. The period of transition from infatuations to realistic peer relationships involves learning, through frequent real-life interactions with girls,

about what society expects from young men and women, and about the range and variety of people and situations. Sometimes the transition between fantasy and reality is painful, and a boy must contend with rejection.

Situation

Tom saves Sara's cat from drowning by jumping into the stream and pulling the cat out. Tom has always admired Sara from a (safe) distance; Sara has never known about Tom's crush on her. How will Sara react to Tom's act of bravery? Will she now be in love with him? Or may she be merely grateful, and perhaps try to repay him by inviting him over or buying him a gift?

In fact, there is no reason why Sara should fall in love with Tom. His act of heroism may inspire gratitude or admiration, but not necessarily love. Sara's response of appreciation may be misread by Tom as a sign of affection or love. He will soon learn, however, of her true feelings: she likes him as a person, feels thankful for his action, but has not fallen in love.

■■■■

Girls' behavior is often misinterpreted by boys, but eventually boys become better able to "read" girls' true feelings and intentions—at least some of the time. The example of Tom and Sara demonstrates that an act of physical strength and bravery is not usually the basis for an affectionate or loving relationship, although it can be a part of one. Boys and girls usually develop relationships built on mutual respect, understanding, and shared interests.

Situation

Larry and Diana both play musical instruments for the school orchestra. One afternoon, practice runs late, and Diana cannot reach her mother to get a ride home. She will have to carry her cello all the way home. Larry offers to carry her cello, and Diana accepts gladly. Once home, Larry tells Diana that he'll carry the instrument back to school the next morning. On the way to school,

Larry asks Diana if she'd like to go with him to a special concert on Saturday afternoon. Diana is pleased and accepts. Over the next few months, they see each other two or three times a week, spend time together practicing their music, and often do other things they both enjoy.

———

Larry and Diana's relationship is built not on a single act of bravery or physical strength, but on enduring interests (in music) and shared experiences (in other activities).

As a boy matures, he shows more signs of interest in girls his own age. These feelings may come and go, perhaps as his interests in sports or other activities change, or maybe as his group of friends puts more or less pressure on him to remain involved solely with them.

Peer pressure

"All the guys enjoy making fun of Tara, and I follow along. I feel bad because I like her a lot and never told anyone. I am sure the guys would get on me if I said anything. It's hard deciding between the gang and her."

When friends get you to go along with their decisions (even if you're not quite sure you want to), it's called *peer pressure*. Boys during early adolescence and later are under a lot of pressure to go along with the gang. During this stage, the group is very important. Boys feel most secure with other males, especially in a group. The dilemma of choosing between the accepted behavior of the other kids in the group and new interests (i.e. girls) is common, especially if a boy is not the leader or if no one else in the group has a girlfriend. No one wants to be the first to be different. Also, a boy who is sure of the gang's loyalty may not feel sure he wants to risk losing that for a girl who may not even like him. In most cases a younger, less confident boy will decide to stay with "the guys" and go along with the already accepted treatment of girls (ignoring or teasing them). Boys may even make snide and cruel remarks towards girls, just to show that they are "superior." Boys at this age attempt to feel superior because underneath they may feel very inferior. They may be physically smaller than some girls, and may also be frightened about new changes and feelings they are experiencing. Rather than face these new feelings they attempt to ignore or mask them. As boys grow up, they learn to balance their need for same-sex friends and opposite-sex friends.

Peer information about love

Being part of a group at this age is important for a boy. He needs constant contact with his friends, and he needs their approval for most things he does. The group has rules and regulations and you have to abide by them, if you want to be a part of the group. Besides serving as a support group, individuals in the group also serve as sources of information.

The problem with information given by friends of the same age and same sex is that it is very limited, and may in fact be false. Peers may lack knowledge and experience, and a boy's friends may not have any better sources of information than he has. Yet, because group loyalty is strong, *everything* that other members of the group say tends to be regarded as the truth. Often the information is passed on by ill-informed older friends and brothers, or false impressions are formed by television and movies.

This misinformation often includes, of course, "facts" about sex, girls, love, and how to be a "real man." This is why such myths as "males must be strong and silent" or "men who show tender feelings are weak" or "if a girl gets pregnant it's her own fault" continue to

be believed. Boys need to hear what kind of masculine behavior girls admire from girls—not from other boys.

Boys are getting the message today that it is okay to be tender and show other feelings. There is no longer a rigid definition of manhood. Boys are even permitting girls to be part of their groups and are finding that when they treat girls equally, the transition into dating is not quite so startling or painful. As boys get older and gain more experience, they begin to get better information from more reliable sources such as informed adults, books, or teachers.

Love and embarrassment

At about the same time that boys are beginning to notice girls, their bodies are going through dramatic physiological changes. These changes can cause many embarrassing moments.

"As I was asking her to the dance, I realized that I was sweating a lot. I don't know if she noticed, but I felt like a jerk."

"We talked for the first time on the telephone yesterday. Right in the middle of the conversation, my voice cracked. I sounded like my little brother. I couldn't wait to hang up."

"All I was doing was talking to her. I wasn't thinking about sex or anything and I got an erection. I don't know if she could tell. I could have died."

"You know, my feet are so big that sometimes I don't think I can control them. As I helped her pick up her books during recess, I tripped and fell flat on my face—right in front of everyone."

"I tried to impress her by lifting my bike out of the rack with one hand. As I did, I ripped my shirt."

"She asked me about the bandage on my face. I couldn't tell her I cut myself shaving—I only have a few hairs and she would have thought I was being ridiculous. So I lied."

These experiences, painful as they may be, are part of growing up. Sweaty palms, clumsy feet, cracking voices—often these responses just cannot be controlled. Most girls don't notice these reactions; or if they do, they don't judge a boy because of them. As a boy grows older he understands that there is no need to perform perfectly all the time. The most important thing is being himself.

Parental pressures and expectations

Parents may try to delay their son's developing interest in or activities with girls. They may be confused and worried as they watch their son mature and express his need for independence. They may be uneasy as they realize that friends sometimes seem more important to him than family. They may nag him:

☐ How can you get your homework done if you stay out every evening with her?

☐ You know we have plans for your future. Don't mess them up by getting girl-crazy.

☐ Do you always have to see the same girl?

☐ Bring her home; we'd like to meet her. What does her father do for a living.

A boy may think his parents are overreacting. "We're not getting married—we're just going to the game with each other!" he might protest. In many cases parents' concerns are honest ones. They know that sometimes it's hard to keep a clear perspective about an infatuation or relationship, and they may be anxious to protect their son against being hurt or rejected. Still, in most cases, a boy needs and deserves all the privacy and support his parents can give him.

Other boys may feel that they are being pushed by one or both parents into discussing their feelings about girls. They may resent repeated questions ("So, do you have a girl yet?") or teasing comments ("I saw you walking with Melissa today—is she your girlfriend all of a sudden?"). Most boys can handle these remarks, by responding with a simple yes or no, or ignoring them. They can remind their parents that they have to move at their own pace, especially when it comes to dating.

If your parents are pressuring you one way or another about girls, you might want to sit down and talk to them about it. You can probably satisfy their concerns by saying something like "Carly and I aren't getting too serious, so don't worry about me getting overinvolved. We just enjoy each other's company" or "You really make me uncomfortable when you tease me about Melissa." They should respect your wishes.

He said that she said . . .

The games boys and girls play that deal with emotions and feelings can cause important problems during this period. Sometimes, for instance, young people gossip or tell stories about each other. Some of these stories could be true, while others are definitely false. Some rumors can get young people in trouble and cause real unhappiness.

Situation

The other day during history class, someone passed around a note that said *Lisa A. Loves Jason R.* When Lisa saw it she felt so embarrassed she wanted to cry. The truth was, she was thinking that Jason was cute, but she also liked another boy. She wasn't sure which boy she liked better.

The same day during music class, someone passed around a note that said *Jason wants to make it with Lisa.* Jason felt confused when he saw it. He was angry at whoever had started the rumor and sad because he really liked Lisa and the note was insulting to her. He was unsure how to act in front of his friends: would denying it make them believe it even more, or would ignoring it make them think it was true? He wondered if he should laugh about it with them. He felt there was nothing he could really do.

Now when Lisa and Jason pass each other in the hall, they don't look at each other. Jason had been planning to go to a certain party because he was looking forward to seeing Lisa there. He thinks he'd better not go because it might be awkward for both of them.

Whoever sent those notes may have thought it was a funny or harmless prank. In fact, it caused a misunderstanding between Lisa and Jason, and hurt the feelings of each of them. It may have ruined a friendship or created a false image of someone. So think carefully before you start or spread rumors—would you like to be at the other end?

Different strokes for different folks

When boys are just beginning to notice girls, they find it hard to express their feelings for them.

Situation

Blake and Gerry are friends. Blake is big for his age and has been interested in girls for about a year. Gerry sometimes calls Blake "girl-crazy." Gerry is average for his age and is not sure how to act around girls. One moment he likes them and the next moment he would rather not think of them.

Gerry and Blake begin to like two girls who hang around together. Every time that Blake sees them he tries to get Gerry to go over and talk with them. Gerry usually finds an excuse not to. Blake often responds by going himself. This begins to put a strain on their friendship. Often Gerry does want to talk with them but is unsure of himself. He cannot understand how Blake can do it so easily. The more Blake pushes Gerry, the more uncomfortable each of them feels. This continues until Blake feels that Gerry is holding him back, and Gerry feels resentful of Blake's ease with girls. The two no longer hang around together.

━━━

The boys in this situation are moving at different paces. Both are normal. Every young man matures at his own rate: nothing can speed it up. Perhaps Blake should be able to proceed while respecting Gerry's need not to move too fast. It might help for them to talk it over together.

BLAKE You coming to the movies tonight? Ellen and her friend are going.

GERRY Listen, Blake, why don't you just meet Ellen at the movies? I mean, you want to be alone with her and I don't want to be alone with her friend. She's okay but I'm just not interested in any girl.

BLAKE But Ellen's friend asked if you were coming. What should I say?

GERRY Just tell her I had other plans. You should go by yourself. Honestly, I'm just not interested. I don't want to hurt her feelings—or yours, or anybody's.

BLAKE So what will you do tonight?

GERRY   I thought I'd go to the gym and throw a few
    baskets. Maybe you can catch me there later.

BLAKE   Okay, if you're sure. We'll see you later.

In this conversation, it's clear that Blake is a little
anxious about meeting Ellen and would like to have
Gerry along. Also, he is worried about what Gerry will
do, since they usually spend time together that he is
now spending with Ellen. Gerry indicates that he
doesn't want to be pushed into dating, yet he understands how Blake is feeling. It's okay for Blake to pur-
sue his interest in Ellen and for Gerry to do something
else—they can still be friends.

Man to man: same-sex relationships and love

A boy may feel pressured to enter into boy-girl relationships by his parents, his friends, or a girl who likes
him. If he feels that he isn't ready, he should not let
himself be pushed.

People may pressure him for many reasons: parents
may do it to try to make sure their son doesn't become
a homosexual; male friends because they think it is
what they are supposed to do for each other; or girls
because they think a boy may be a "good catch."

Parents' fear of homosexuality is usually based on
their own insecurities and fears about sexuality. They
may think that their son is too close to his best friend.
And they may be convinced that unless he has a girlfriend soon, the male relationship will turn into a homosexual relationship. If a boy isn't athletic or sports-
minded, parents sometimes become even more
concerned.

During the middle school years boys develop close
same-sex relationships and some experimentation
takes place within the relationship. This is normal
and part of growing up. It doesn't mean a boy is going
to become homosexual. Homosexuality isn't *caused* by

close same-sex friendships or a lack of interest in sports. The development of sexual preference is a complex process, resulting from many factors in one's life.

People's fear of homosexuality is reflected in how they use the label "homosexual." We know that the worst name one boy can call another is "fag" or "faggot" or "gay." It is considered a real attack or insult. However, calling other people names usually reflects the insecurities of the person who needs to taunt or label others.

Male-to-male relationships are very important in the life cycle of men. Love can be a part of those relationships. Males feel very badly when their best friend is hurt or has problems. They can be tender and caring with each other, and they need the comfort that each gives to the other. If a boy has a close friend, that friendship should be respected, not regarded as weird or suspicious.

Roles and role models: mixed messages

Girls and boys learn to behave as adult women and men by observing adults; from reading books for pleasure; from studying history, science, literature, art; and from the media (movies, theater, television, magazines, and advertising). They learn from role models, by observing and copying those people they look up to. Mothers, grandmothers, aunts, and sisters are natural role models for girls. Fathers, grandfathers, uncles, and brothers are role models for boys. As children mature, they also look to their teachers, favorite performers, and other significant adults.

Today girls are being educated so that they can compete in the job market as doctors, lawyers, construction workers, and other fields that have traditionally been reserved for men. Girls often feel a conflict between traditional and nontraditional roles and behavior—between what they learn intellectually about new

56

opportunities and roles, and what they observe in the women around them. So a girl may assert herself in sports, but still be very passive when on a date. A girl may be treated as an equal to boys at school, but may be expected to behave more traditionally (to be subservient and nurturing) at home. At school girls may be able to take industrial arts, but at home they may be expected to cook and clean rather than fix the lawnmower. Although she may think it is perfectly normal to invite a boy on a date, a girl may be expected to stay in while her brother is free to go out alone. Some television programs and advertisers feature women as forceful and powerful while some continue to characterize women as dumb, frivolous, important only as caretakers (cooking, cleaning, taking care of children) or sex objects. Many manufacturers continue to exploit women's bodies in order to sell products.

Boys have also received confusing and conflicting messages about traditional and nontraditional expectations. Boys are being educated in nontraditional fields, such as secretarial work, dancing, nursing, child care. The male stereotype (strong, silent, always in control) is being replaced by a more open, caring male hero; but boys are still often criticized by peers, older males, or their families when they express their feelings. If a boy cries because he is sad or hurt, or if he hugs or embraces another boy when he is happy, he will still be called names like "sissy," "mama's boy," "fag."

Traditionally, men were expected to be sexually knowledgeable and experienced while girls remained pure and innocent. In order to be "manly" a boy was supposed to use and manipulate girls. Today boys may actively avoid experimenting with girls or pretending they have feelings for a girl just to get her to make out. Yet they still feel anxious or inadequate if they don't initiate physical contact, or if a girl glimpses vulnerable or uncertain feelings.

Friends can help boys feel less anxious by support-
ing their efforts to change. You can compliment a
friend when he is open and honest ("I'm really glad
you're able to tell me how you feel") and make it clear
that the old masculine stereotype is not attractive ("I
don't think trying to insult someone by calling them
gay is very smart" or "I love to watch my brother care
for his new baby"). Girls have always had more freedom to hold hands and kiss or hug each other. If the
sexes are to be equal, boys should have this freedom
too. By being aware of what influences our behavior,
we may be liberating ourselves from feeling restricted,
tense, or unhappy.

III. For Boys about Girls

Dear Beth,

My boyfriend goes away to school. When he's home, we
sometimes go out on a date, or he'll come over to my
house for awhile. I love him so much it hurts! I don't
think he knows. I have these fantasies about when we
are married and everything. We write and I always sign
my letters "love," and so does he, but it's not the same
as saying "I love you." Sometimes I want to tell him
how much I care, but they say the guy should say it
first.

Madly in Love with C.S.

■

Dear Madly in Love,

There is no reason why a girl can't say "I love you," if
it's true. There's no reason a girl can't ask a boy out,
and by college age, many girls are able to do this. Most
younger girls, however—even those who say it is okay
in theory—never actually do speak first. Girls in the
past were not supposed to be so assertive, and they still
fear boys wouldn't like it. This isn't necessarily so.

Even if you don't feel comfortable speaking or calling
first, it doesn't mean you have to sit passively and wait.

Through history, girls have found ways to let boys know how they feel. They do it by direct or indirect hints, by discussions or theoretical cases: "Suppose a girl loved a boy and didn't know how he felt. What should she do?" They get friends to pass the word. They comment on other kids' relationships, to try to give their boyfriends the message.

Girls tend to romanticize, daydreaming, as you do, about marriage. Boys' fantasies are more apt to concern the more physical aspects. They aren't as anxious to be tied down.

Proof of how people feel can best be found in the ways they treat each other. Does this boy write often? Does he spend as much time as possible with you when he's home? Is he very attentive to you when he's with you? If so, you can feel sure he cares, even if he doesn't put it into words.

Beth

■

Ten Love Dilemmas

1. Giant steps

"My parents don't like my boyfriend. My dad says that he's not good enough for me. It's just that my boyfriend is shy and whenever they're alone with him, my boyfriend doesn't say anything."

When a girl starts to date, her family is bound to have some reactions. Sisters may give advice on how to behave and how to dress; they can be supportive and understanding, or critical and domineering. Little brothers may tease a girl about having a boyfriend, perhaps because they are jealous of the new man in her life. Older brothers may be a good source of guidance and advice since they've been through the experience from the other side. Ideally, mothers and daughters will feel comfortable discussing the new

emotions and feelings a girl is experiencing. Some mothers may be happy, and recollecting their own early dating experiences may be fun for both mother and daughter. Some mothers, however, may worry a lot and hope they can protect their daughters from making mistakes. Fathers may give their daughters mixed messages about boys, love, and dating. A father may feel proud that his daughter is maturing, but the fact that she is becoming a woman may also make him a bit nervous. He may be more comfortable discussing school and sports than her "love life."

Some girls may resent others' advice and prefer to rely on their own experience. But while it may be true that "experience is the best teacher," listening to advice in the area of love and dating can really help.

Beginning to date and form intimate friendships outside your family is kind of like the game Giant Steps. It is a gradual process of starting and stopping. (You may take *one giant step forward:* go out to dinner on a date. You must take *three baby steps backward:* choose to spend New Year's Eve with your family instead of at a boy/girl party.) On the same weekend a girl may go to an eighth-grade dance with a boy, and spend the next day jumping rope with friends. A boy may see a girl a lot in one week, but the next week feel like spending time with "the guys" again.

During the process of gaining independence and moving out into the world on your own, you need the chance to go forward, try the unknown, and separate from family, as well as to move back periodically to family and the known. It helps if your family understands that just because you have a special friend now, you won't necessarily always have or want one.

There are some things that a boy can do to help a girl's family accept the fact that she is dating:

☐ He can be on time to pick her up.
☐ He can come to the door rather than sit in the car and beep the horn.
☐ He can stand up and shake hands when her parents come into the room.
☐ He can try (before he arrives at the house) to think of a question to ask her father or mother, such as "Who do you think will win the baseball game?" or "I notice you've been working on the house—are you doing the work yourself?"
☐ If he's feeling nervous, he should keep in mind that family members are too!

It may seem artificial to have to make yourself do these things, but after a few times the atmosphere will be more relaxed. Girls will appreciate your efforts, and this is bound to improve the relationship all around.

2. Love and drugs don't mix

"I really like this boy, but I know he takes drugs—I think he smokes pot once or twice a week. I wish he didn't but I'm not sure if I should say anything to him about it."

A girl may be concerned about dating a boy who uses drugs. She may worry about how a boy will act if he's stoned or drunk; she may wonder if he will behave differently than he does when she sees him at school. She may be afraid she'll be pressured into trying something she isn't ready for. She may worry about getting into legal trouble.

An important reason for a girl to be concerned about a boy who uses drugs is the question of *why* he is involved with drugs. If he can't have a good time without drugs, he may be covering up insecurities or other problems. If he does it because everyone else does, he probably isn't very independent. Girls like to know the real person—but drugs disguise him.

3. Experimentation

"I've had seven boyfriends in seven months. My friends say I'm crazy and that I use boys, but I just keep changing my mind."

What's reasonable? What is the double standard and does it still exist? The double standard means that there is one behavior code for girls and another for boys. Girls are expected to be passive, innocent, and naive. Boys are expected to be aggressive, assertive, and experienced in love. The double standard *does* still exist and causes problems for girls. Traditionally, boys were given indirect or unstated permission to experiment with girls by having a number of various sexual experiences during adolescence. Girls were taught that it was wrong and immoral for them to experience sexual feelings, and that if they did experiment with boys, they would get a bad reputation that would deter nice boys. Times have changed, and the women's liberation movement has helped make things more equal. But girls are still not as free as boys to express themselves physically. Of course, one of the foundations of the double standard is the fact that if girls try to explore their sexual feelings with boys they can get pregnant. It is important for girls—and boys—to be cautious and careful about the physical expression of love. It is best to wait until you develop a good sense of trust and understanding, and until you are well informed about the consequences of any decisions. However, there is nothing wrong with a girl having a few different boyfriends during the year, as this is part of discovering the qualities of a more long-lasting relationship.

4. Getting hurt—guilt and shame

"I'm only in the eighth grade. I broke up with this boy who I really loved. I really thought I could trust him. I wish I'd waited because now I worry all the time about what he's saying about me. How could I have been such a fool? I never want another boyfriend—ever!"

Girls still worry a lot about what others will say about them. Each individual must set her own standards. Taking time to get to know a person is very important before you do anything you might later be uncomfortable or worried about.

If a girl does something she later regrets, she may experience more guilt than a boy would in the same situation. She may feel ashamed or embarrassed about how she behaved. She will think about what happened for a long time and feel sad or depressed.

One way to help girls avoid this is for a boy to refrain from talking about a girl while and after they are dating. In this way he can show respect for their private relationship. A boy who needs to brag may not realize how much he is hurting the girl. Another way a boy can help is to be willing to date a girl who may have had a difficult experience with another boy. He can be patient and understanding. He can let her know that he respects her in all ways. Friends can help a girl by letting her know that she is still a good person (who made a mistake) and encouraging her not to be too hard on herself. She may still have some regrets, but she may also be able to benefit from the experience. Learning about love requires risking . . . and risking can mean getting hurt. It can also mean learning a lot about yourself.

5. Trust your instincts

"I'm not really interested in boys. I mean, I like them but I have more fun with girls. I can relax and act the way I want. So sometimes I pretend that I'm thinking about boys while the other girls are talking about them. And my parents are always saying stupid things like 'How's your boyfriend?' when I don't even have or want one. I wonder if there's something wrong with me."

Lots of girls feel pressured into dating by other girls, boys, their family, and other adults. A girl should just be herself; if she's not interested, she should try to ignore the pressure.

Why do others assume, just because a girl looks as if she is maturing, that she should have a boyfriend? One reason may be that others get anxious about sexual orientation. A parent may want a girl to date to prove that she's "normal," i.e. heterosexual. They may project their fear, even at a very early age, that she'll grow up without a boyfriend or husband or companion and will be lonely or unfulfilled later on. Girls may also tease each other or call one another "les" (short for lesbian). Nevertheless, no girl should have to prove that she is feminine, especially not by dating. Everyone is anxious or nervous about what the future holds, but nobody should pressure you or hurt your feelings because of their own fears or insecurities.

Here is a list of five wrong reasons for dating:

1. All the other girls are.
2. You think you have to prove yourself as a woman.

3. Your parents are pushing you.
4. Your brothers and sisters are teasing you.
5. You think you aren't normal for not being interested.

There is no reason to rush into dating. Some girls do not date or have a steady relationship with a boy until they are in their twenties. They may think about boys but not meet one they really like; or they may just be busy with other activities—studies, sports, a career—for a while.

A girl's friendships with other girls are very important, just as a boy's friendships with other boys are. Her relationships with other girls are a foundation for future relationships of all kinds. With other girls she can enjoy talking about books, seeing movies, participating in sports, thinking about education and career goals, discussing family problems, dreaming about the future, being silly and having fun.

When a girl is ready to have an intimate boyfriend, she can continue to enjoy friends who are boys and friends who are girls. In fact, this is an important clue: if you also enjoy other girl and boy friendships, you are probably in a healthy, mature relationship with your boyfriend.

What are the qualities of a good relationship? First, consider what to avoid. A boy may not be right for a girl if:

☐ He is much older.
☐ He thinks he is cool because he uses drugs, liquor, or cigarettes.
☐ He has hurt other girls' feelings.
☐ She has to sneak to go out with him.
☐ He asks her to do things that she feels uncomfortable about.

By contrast, a good relationship begins when:

☐ She enjoys being with him because they have many common interests.
☐ He respects her.

☐ He is sensitive to her needs.
☐ He is comfortable with her, her friends, and her family.
☐ He is easy to talk to.

6. Communication—a two-way street

"I really like this boy but as soon as we are alone— I'm speechless! I don't know what to say. My mind goes blank."

When it comes to love, every emotion is involved and communication is the key. Everyone knows something about communicating—how to say hello, make conversation, figure out whether the other person is listening or what he or she is feeling. We do this every day with friends, parents, and teachers. But there are new dimensions of communication in a special friendship. At first, feelings of excitement, nervousness, and the unknown are part of getting to know the other person. You each learn new ways to communicate.

In a good relationship, both people must work consistently to improve communication. They must learn to express themselves honestly, and they must not be afraid to show the good feelings as well as the difficult ones. You may have to encourage a girl to show her honest feelings by being honest yourself, and this can be difficult or scary in the beginning. Sometimes it's harder to communicate certain feelings than to express others, and you should recognize what feelings your friend struggles with. Boys may find it easier to show anger than to show sadness. Girls may find it easier to show helplessness than to show anger.

A good relationship will be built on sharing positive feelings. A girl will not know you admire her sensitivity with other people unless you tell her. She will not know that you feel a little inadequate or nervous at times with adults unless you tell her. Sometimes you can tell people how you feel through nonverbal com-

67

munication—you can send a gift, or give a hug, or dedicate a poem or project to them.

7. Infatuation

"I have a crush on this guy. He's a lifeguard at the pool. He's too old for me, I know, but. . . ."

Yes, lots of girls have crushes—on older boys, younger boys, teachers, movie stars, and singers. When a girl has a crush on someone, she probably thinks about him a lot. He may be someone she knows she cannot "have" or most likely will not "get." She wonders at times if he even knows she is alive. When she sees him, she may feel her heart beat faster; her knees may get weak; and her stomach may be all butterflies. And she may do some pretty goofy things, like wander by his home several times a day, or after he has walked by, go stand where his feet touched the ground—just to imagine being closer to him. Silly? Yes. Normal? Yes.

In a way, having crushes is a way for a girl to prepare for the time when she really has a boyfriend. She acts the situation out in her mind so that when the real thing happens, she will know what to do. There probably is some comfort for her in knowing she cannot really have him, although at the time she thinks he is all she'll ever want.

8. Just friends

"I've been going with this boy, but now he gets mad when I talk to my old friends, boys I've known all my life."

Throughout life, having friends of both the same and the opposite sex is important. Even when a girl has begun dating a special boy, her friendships with other boys continue. Her relationships with others should enhance her relationship with an intimate friend, because she has the opportunity to discuss common interests, feelings, and concerns with other boys and girls—and because no one person can satisfy all of another's needs. This type of friendship is often called "Platonic love." The phrase refers to the Greek philosopher Plato, who wrote about how a person can love another person in a nonsexual way. A girl who has Platonic friendships will have new ideas and thoughts to enrich her relationship with her closer friend. If a boy tries to make his relationship with a girl too possessive and exclusive of others, he may be too insecure about himself to have a healthy relationship with a girl. Unwarranted jealousy can end a relationship quickly.

9. Beauty is in the eyes of the beholder

"Do you think we can't hear them? 'Check her out! That ain't bad! I wouldn't throw her out of my bed!' Is that all boys think about—looks?"

During middle- and high-school years, relationships are often initially based on physical attraction, and the physical attraction is based on looks and appearance. Boys' ideas of "good looks" are often limited to the idealized version defined by magazines and television.

Why are looks so important? One reason is that people measure themselves by those around them. A girl may want to be admired by a particular handsome boy so other girls will think she is a success. A boy may want to be friends with a particular pretty girl so other boys will not put him down. As individuals become more secure and confident about themselves, they are less likely to be concerned about what others think of their choices. When this happens, they begin to look for more important qualities in a person. They begin to define good looks for themselves. They become confident enough to seek a friend whom they really like, not one all the others consider desirable because of his or her looks.

Boys should remember that girls have many of the

same insecurities about their looks as boys have—they worry that they are not pretty enough; that they are too tall or too short, too developed or not developed enough; that their hair is too curly or too straight. You can help each other by learning to appreciate the unique individual qualities of each person through your own perceptions of his or her looks, talents, sensitivity, warmth, sincerity, and interests.

10. Together and apart: endings

"I went with this boy for six months. Then he started to avoid me. I don't think he likes another girl, and I still like him."

It is very hard on a girl when a relationship ends, especially when she has no idea why. Sometimes boys are unable to express their feelings so they just walk away from a relationship without any explanation. This is very unkind and unfair to the girl—and to the boy himself. She feels rejected. Because she doesn't know *why* the relationship is over, she blames herself: I'm not pretty enough, I did something to upset him, I'm not a good person. It may take her a long time to feel good about herself again, and she may feel too sad and depressed to go on and make other friendships. Boys may feel at the time that an abrupt ending is easier, but inside they know it isn't fair or honest.

A boy may have any of several reasons he should share with the girl:

□ He was feeling too tied down.
□ He wanted more time alone.
□ He wanted more times with other friends.
□ He realized he wasn't ready for a serious, intimate relationship.

He may still feel that she is a good friend and a talented, attractive person. However, if he has his own reasons for wanting to break up, he must tell her.

Sadness

Dear Beth,

My mom and dad are splitting up. I am going to live with my mother. I want to live with her, but I'm afraid dad will feel hurt. He's going to have an apartment, and I will visit him on weekends, but he will be alone all week. It seems so unfair, it makes me want to cry. I think about this all the time. Mom says he will see his friends, but he says he will miss us a lot.

Sad Sack

Dear Sad Sack,

Your concern for your father is kind and loving. You worry about him missing you, but you are also sad because you are going to miss him. Children always feel sad when their parents divorce, and usually wish they could stay together and be a happy family, even though things were not that happy before.

Most kids feel many emotions at this time: anger at their parents for separating, fear of what their future will be like, guilt that it may be their fault, shame about what other kids may think, grief over the loss of daily contact with one parent. You feel badly every time you think about what you have lost. Crying is one way to relieve such feelings, for men and boys as well as for

71

women and girls. Talking about it to others helps, too. You carry this big lump of sadness around for awhile, but then as time passes, the memories no longer make you so intensely unhappy. Your life fills up again. Perhaps being alone with your father will bring you even closer than you were before. You can talk to him on the phone between visits.

Sadness and loss happen to everyone from time to time. Learning to work through it, with optimism that you will feel better soon, is a helpful lesson in growing up.

Beth

■

Dear Beth,

Josie is my best friend. We do everything together—rollerskating, biking, swimming, walking back and forth from school. We've been friends since we were five years old.

Last week her father got a promotion and now her family is going to move to Texas as soon as school gets out in June. Now when we're together, we're just sad all of the time. Also, it makes me mad because I think her parents aren't being fair; they're just acting happy all the time like everything is wonderful.

Sad Carrie

■

Dear Carrie,

Having your best friend move far away is one of the saddest things that can happen. We are often the most sad (and mad!) when things happen to us—things which we cannot control and cannot change.

Her parents are probably sad, too, about leaving their friends. They may even know how she feels, but they want to act happy and enthusiastic about their new home so she'll feel happier.

Maybe you could prepare for the time when your friend is moving by doing things—like making stationery for each other or thinking of something special to exchange to remember each other by. Perhaps you can even discuss with your parents possible plans for summer visits to each other's houses.

Beth

Why is it that each time you feel sad, it seems as if it is the first time and it feels as if it is never going to end? When you think about it later, even though there were different reasons, you realize it is the same sad feeling. But when you are in the feeling, you are sure you have never felt this way before.

Identifying when we are sad

Sad gets mixed up with other emotions, and so with each new experience it feels a little bit different:

☐ When your favorite apple tree is struck by lightning during a hurricane, it is sad.

☐ It is very, very sad when your dog or your cat dies.

☐ You can feel sad when a movie ends because it reminds you of an experience you have had.

☐ You can feel sad when you have to move away from your friends.

☐ A particular kind of a day can create a sad mood for you—a gray, cloudy day; a rainy, drizzly day; even, surprisingly, a blue-sky day.

☐ When you are home alone or when your parents go away on a trip, you may feel sad even though you thought you would not miss them.

☐ You can really be enjoying camp, or biking, or a canoe trip, and suddenly feel very sad and very lonesome.

So sadness may be mixed with helplessness or loneliness; feeling sad may mean feeling hopeless, distant, or homesick.

Here are some expressions that mean the same as *sad:*

heavy-hearted	blue	down in the
feeling down	in the doldrums	dumps
low in spirits	feeling like a	showing a long
	sourpuss	face
		broken-hearted
		crushed

What do you do when you are sad?

People express sadness in many different ways. You or your friend may want time alone to think quietly about what has happened. Or you may want time to-gether to talk about the sadness. When you are sad, you may want to listen to music, paint or draw, write a poem, keep a journal, or bake cookies.

Crying is often an expression of sadness or hurt. You may want to be alone when you are sad. Some-times you withdraw and that is okay for a little while. Being alone with sadness may be one person's way of coping—of experiencing the feeling inside, alone.

The physiology of emotions

Did you ever wonder what happens in your body to bring on tears? You can cry as a result of several dif-ferent feelings. For example, Sad Sack wanted to cry because he felt that it was unfair that his dad was alone during the week. Those were tears of sadness. Have you ever laughed so long and so hard that tears came to your eyes? Why do people cry at weddings? They may not feel sad and they probably don't think it is funny. So tears can be an expression of several dif-ferent emotions, including sadness, excitement, and elation.

Here are some other physical reactions when you are sad:

1. Your heart begins to pound.
2. Your pulse begins to race.
3. Your hands become damp and clammy.
4. You may experience a feeling of nausea.
5. The blood leaves your stomach.
6. The blood rushes to your heart, brain, and muscles.

Your body may also react in the same way for other strong emotions, such as anger, worry, fear, or dread.

Kids talk about what makes them sad

JOSH My parents are divorced and sometimes when I'm with one, I suddenly think about the other, and I'll feel sad and wonder how he's feeling, or what she's doing.

TINA My friend's grandmother died when we were in the fifth grade. She cried and cried that night. But her sister didn't cry. Her brother looked like he'd been crying. My mother said he probably did cry sometimes when he was alone.

SEAN Once I saw my mother cry. I didn't know what to do. I mean, I know mothers, people cry. But I had never seen my mother cry.

KIM I feel really sad when I see a kid who's crippled. And I don't want to stare, but I don't want to look away either.

ROLAND When I'm alone at night and watching a really sad movie, I can bawl my eyes out! I wonder why things in a movie can make me sadder than real life sometimes.

Kim describes how she feels when she sees a person who is handicapped. Her response is a mixture of awkwardness, curiosity, sadness, and helplessness. Part of her response may be due to imagining how she would feel if she were the other person. This is a natural response. If she can sort out her feelings, she will find it easier to react comfortably. Her interactions with a disabled person will be more natural, which is what most handicapped persons desire.

Roland is bewildered because he is able to cry his eyes out when he watches movies and wonders why he appears more affected by a movie than by real-life situations. When you are alone, it may be easier to release emotions by crying. This release, really letting go, is healthy and can allow you to explore your inner feelings. When you are with others, two things may happen: you may be more inhibited about showing your feelings in the presence of another person; or you may hold back in a real-life situation because you do not know the depth of the emotion. It may feel bottomless, endless, boundless. It may seem too scary, so you may attempt to keep it under control.

Having empathy

To express sympathy means to share in suffering or grieving; if someone has experienced a loss, you can offer them your sympathy. Empathy is something you feel inside. Empathy is the ability to project your consciousness into another person, to feel what another person is feeling. Empathy is a quality, a part of your personality that you develop as you mature. Because you can imagine how another is going to feel, you can think before you act—knowing what the possible consequences of your actions or words will be. When a three-year-old hits another three-year-old with a toy truck, the three-year-old cannot be expected to feel how much it hurts the other child. But if you have a friend who has just failed an exam, you are able to understand how unhappy she must feel because you can imagine how unhappy you'd feel. You gradually become empathetic. You may experience a little or a lot of empathy, depending on how close you are to the other person who is feeling hurt or sad. Having empathy means being very sensitive to how another person is feeling. Having empathy also shows that you are a good observer and a good listener.

Boys and sadness/girls and sadness

In a study about feelings, two groups of boys and girls, ages thirteen to fifteen and sixteen to eighteen, were asked how they felt when a tragedy occurred to one of their friends. Of the boys, 80 percent said they felt sad, too; 92 percent of the girls felt sad. In both the younger and the older groups, more girls than boys experienced sadness. Does this mean that females are slightly more empathetic than males in our society? The researchers felt that the main sex difference—the difference between the ways males and females react to sadness—comes in coping with it and expressing it. Boys are still more likely to attempt either to avoid feeling sad or to avoid expressing their sadness. Yet the study showed that the great majority of young people in our society, both males and females, are empathetic.

Another interesting result of this study was to compare the reactions of American youth with those of youth from other countries. This is called a cross-cultural study. Youth in the other cultures (Australia, Ireland, and Israel) were asked to respond to the same question about tragedy occurring to one of their friends:

Americans 1970s	Americans 1960s	Australians	Irish	Israelis
88%	89%	89%	88%	88%

There was no difference among the nationalities.

For Girls about Boys

Boys are very likely to want to be alone with their sadness. Or they may like to be distracted from the sadness by occupying themselves with an activity. Try responding to your friend accordingly. If he wants to be alone, leave him be. If he wants company, know that he may truly want to do anything to take his mind off the sad feeling—for a while, anyway.

Sometimes, what a boy likes to read about may give you a hint about how he copes with sadness. Many boys enjoy science fiction and adventure stories: the central characters in these books are often involved in solitary pursuits and are not much concerned with relationships with other people. Although the character may be alone, he is not portrayed as lonely or needy, but as strong, self-reliant, and attractive. This kind of characterization reinforces some boys' tendency to avoid directly dealing with their feelings.

Sometimes, however, a boy may want very much to discuss his feelings and may need only some gentle encouragement to do so. You might tell him about a sad experience your brother went through, for instance, or about a character's experience in a novel. This may help him know you can listen if he wants to talk about his feelings.

For Boys about Girls

Girls may be more comfortable and more willing to experience their sadness in front of others. When a girl is feeling sad, she may need to just be with friends; or to cry, be held, or sit peacefully with another in silence; or to talk. She may be less likely to want to be alone than a boy might, but she also may want to do things to distract herself. Because girls are allowed to cry, or to ask to be comforted—society doesn't view these behaviors as odd or undesirable in women—girls may find sadness one of the simplest emotions to ex-

press. However, that doesn't mean that they don't experience sadness as intensely or deeply as boys.

Reading habits may also offer clues as to how girls cope with sadness. Many girls read novels which have sad and tragic endings, including tales of loneliness, loss, rejection, and longing. Through these stories, girls experience a range of emotions vicariously, which means they imagine themselves in the roles of the characters in the stories. By empathizing with the characters' sad experiences and by reacting (by crying, thinking, talking), girls become slightly more accustomed to dealing with sadness.

Sadness and anger—can they go together?

Yes. For instance, maybe you are feeling a friend's sadness (being empathetic) and your friend will not let you help. Maybe your friend does not know how to trust you, to accept help from you. For just a moment, you might feel anger toward your friend.

Another time anger gets mixed with sadness is when a person very close, a parent or a friend, dies. Combined with the sadness and grief, you may not

only feel anger, you may be furious—at the world, at the person who abandoned you. Part of that feeling is a normal selfish reaction, maybe even toward the person who has died. "How can you abandon me?" "How can this happen to me?" "It is not fair!"

There are many kinds of sadness you can feel—

☐ A sadness that comes and goes.
☐ A timeless sadness that goes on and on.
☐ An incredibly deep sadness.
☐ An uncontrolled sadness.
☐ A mad sadness.
☐ A feeling-sad-and-blue sadness.

Major and minor events make us feel sad. You usually can figure out what specific event is making your friend sad, and time (and understanding) will usually heal that kind of sadness. But frequently grownups and kids can feel sad for long periods of time—days, weeks, even months. They may be moody or distant . . . and they may not know *why* they feel and act sad, cry a lot, or seemed worried all the time. And, in fact, they may be depressed.

Depression

Depression affects people of all ages. When people are depressed, they cannot tell you what is bothering them. They may not understand why they feel the way they do. People who are depressed and sad for no apparent reason need to talk to someone about how they feel. There is a reason, and they must discover it. As a friend, you can encourage a depressed person to talk to someone who has lots of experience—a grandparent, a parent, an aunt, or a teacher they trust. If you are worried about a friend, you might ask your family what you can do to help. Your friend may eventually need to see a professional person, such as a social worker, counselor, or therapist (a "shrink"). If so, try to let your friend know that you will always be a friend; and (maybe without saying it in words) make it known that you think it is a good idea to talk to another person about feelings.

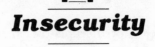

Insecurity

Dear Beth,

I am twelve years old, and not popular in school. All the popular girls get asked out to football games. I only got asked out once. There's this real popular boy who I like. How can I get him to like me? How can I become popular?

Lisa—Ohio

■

Dear Lisa,

More and more, recently, I have received letters from girls who wished they hadn't started dating so young. Being popular is measured by many other things as you get older, not just the number of times you are asked out.

You say you are interested in a very popular boy. This may be a mistake. Try to be realistic and honest with yourself: do you really like him or do you want him because other girls want him? Are you more concerned about the opinion other girls have of you—are you saying to yourself, "If I get him, then everybody will be impressed and realize I'm 'with it' "?

Remember, too, that many boys are still shy. Maybe you'll discover a quieter, less known boy and you can ask *him* to a football game!

If you like yourself, others will like you too. It's no good if you are trying to be something or somebody you aren't. Gradually you'll develop your own style.

Beth

■

Dear Beth,

Last year we moved to this town and in the school here they do a thing called tracking. They put me on a team I didn't like and now I'm going into eighth grade and I'm on the same team again. The kids are okay but all the boys I like are on the other team. I think I'm smart enough to be on that team. My mother says there's nothing we can do about it. Do you think it's fair? I don't know what to do.

Miserable Michael

■

Dear Miserable Michael,

It sounds as if you are working hard to develop a positive self-image and part of that image is to be recognized as being bright and high-achieving. And this is good. Of course, you also want to make sure that you are being realistic about your goals. There may be a reason why your mother thinks there is nothing you can do.

Your mother may not have been encouraged to assert herself when she was your age; if the school makes a decision, she may feel powerless to change it. You could go to your guidance counselor by yourself, explain how you feel, and learn how the decisions are made in your school. If testing has been done, you have a right to ask to see the results. If you are unable to have your team changed, do not let it affect your feelings of self-worth. You can still realize your academic potential, even if you have to do outside work on your own; you may achieve a new sense of satisfaction from your efforts.

Beth

What is insecurity?

Insecurity refers to an emotional state or feeling that is something like worry, but is stronger, deeper, and more personal. When you are feeling insecure, it may be hard to know why you feel the way you do; and if you know why, you may be afraid to admit to anyone what is making you feel insecure.

Each person is a unique emotional individual. Each person has certain experiences that contribute to their feelings of sadness, fear, anger, disappointment, helplessness, pride, and love. But the various degrees of *insecurity*—and its opposite, *security*—are basic to all individuals. If you were to describe any person, you would inevitably comment on their level of security or insecurity. And you'll probably agree that everyone wants to be:

secure	safe	confident
strong	untroubled	self-sufficient
stable	undisturbed	certain

rather than:

insecure	unstable	helpless
weak	disturbed	uncertain
anxious	doubting	dependent

Each person differs regarding the bases of their insecurity and the methods they develop to become more secure. Learning to recognize the source of insecurity is important. Some insecurities will disappear as you get older, but you may have to learn how to overcome other insecurities.

Feelings of insecurity arise from your inner fears and concerns about:

□ Physical growth and development: Am I normal?
□ Beginning dating: How should I act?
□ Family relationships: Where do I fit in my family?
□ Self-image: What kind of person do I want to be?

□ Performance in school, sports, arts: Am I good enough? Smart enough? Talented enough?

Notice that feeling insecure may be related to the emotion of fear, and fear is often based on our feelings about the unknown, the future. Perhaps the biggest question of all, in adolescence, is: *Will I ever grow out of this?*

Masks

You may not be aware of how hidden these concerns are within you. Once you understand how and why you are feeling, you can begin to imagine how others are feeling. You may recognize behaviors that attempt to cover up insecurity; these behaviors can be called masks. Some typical masks:

The Comedian: He may make everybody laugh but inside he is scared that he may not know what to say in a regular conversation with friends, or that people won't like him if he isn't funny or entertaining.

The Scholar: She may have all the answers in math class, but inside she is very uncomfortable in the cafeteria scene where kids are relating and enjoying themselves.

The Smart Aleck: He may act tough but underneath he worries about being accepted in the group.

The Snob: She may act as if she does not like some people but inside she is not sure of herself and worried that they may not like her.

The Know-It-All: He acts as if he has all the answers about everything for everybody else, but inside he does not have the answers for himself.

The Pleaser: She masks her insecurity by constantly pleasing others, by being the teachers' pet and looking for approval from adults.

Everyone needs a mask once in a while. Adolescence is a time of experimentation, of trying out different be-

haviors. Using masks can be part of experimenting. In fact, you may need to pretend to be strong when inside you are really scared. Everyone is insecure the first time they try something new; but after pretending the first few times, you may actually become strong and secure. If someone needs the same mask continually over a long period of time (years), he or she may be hiding some very difficult insecurity, and he or she may need to talk to a counselor or other professional for help.

Physical Growth and Development

Girls: am I normal?

KAREN   I thought I'd never get my period. I was the last girl in the ninth grade to get it.

KATE   Lucky you! I got mine when I was nine. You wouldn't have liked that!

SHARON   I used to hate being so tall. The desks in grammar school were never high enough.

SUSAN How'd you like to be called "shrimp" all the time? And everyone thinks you're younger than you are.

ANNIE Wearing a bra all the time is a drag, especially when you're running or doing gymnastics!

ALISON Well, that's better than having people ask you why you bother to wear one at all . . . or having boys call you "flatso."

LORI I had the biggest feet in the sixth grade. I mean bigger than all the girls *and* the boys. I felt like such a jerk.

LUCY I used to get so mad—I had to buy sandals in the kids' shoe department and there were never any good styles.

BETTE I just about clear up one blemish, and I get another.

BARBARA Now—there's something we agree on. I wish I knew what to do!

Menstruation

Every girl is a little insecure about getting her first period. A girl worries about when she will start menstruating, about how it will feel, and about how she will manage it. It helps to talk honestly with friends. Family and friends can help by assuring her that it is normal for the first menstruation to occur anytime between ages nine and seventeen and that it is normal to have some physical discomfort, such as feeling tired, having cramps, or being moody. Getting information from books and pamphlets can make a girl more comfortable about what's going to happen; she might ask the school nurse or her doctor or look in the library for helpful publications. Family, girl friends, and boyfriends can also help her by respecting her need for additional privacy and by not embarrassing her (for example, about buying sanitary pads or tampons).

87

Breast Size

Body image refers to how a person feels about his or her own body. A person who has a good body image has accepted and is generally pleased with how he or she looks. A person with a poor body image feels negatively about his or her own body or one aspect of his or her body. Developing a positive body image is important to a healthy self-image throughout life. Accepting and feeling good about your breast size and shape is one part of feeling good about yourself as a unique individual. Television and magazines have attempted to make one body type or another more or less desirable. For a time, people thought that women with big breasts were desirable. At another time, women who were flat-chested were presented as attractive. Fortunately, the changing image of women, with less emphasis on sex appeal, has allowed more variety and flexibility, but we are still very much influenced by idealized versions of men and women. The fact is you cannot change the shape or size of your breasts, so it is best to ignore products and exercises that advertise these results. Advertisers who push these products contribute to girls' insecurities about their bodies.

■

Dear Beth,

I am twelve and in seventh grade at a school in San Jose and slightly overweight. Lots of girls are heavier than I am but I don't have that many friends. I know that I would be more confident if I were thinner. *Please* help me! I am especially overweight on my inner thighs.

Sad in S.J.

■

Dear Sad in S.J.,

I get many letters from girls who think they are overweight and who worry especially about their thighs. yourself, affects your confidence. This is true for boys also. Try to build on your strengths and think less about what you believe are your drawbacks. Try to take the initiative in making new friends—reach out rather than waiting for others to come to you.

Beth

■

Weight

Many girls worry that they are either overweight or underweight. In the chapter on Worry there is a table of average heights and weights that may answer some of these concerns. (Keep in mind, however, that those numbers are merely guidelines. The most appropriate weight for you will vary.) Emotion and weight are interrelated for many people. Some people eat a lot when they are upset, others cannot eat at all. Every individual needs a balanced routine of diet and exercise. Naturally, there are times we feel like eating more or less. When a girl goes to an extreme (over- or undereating) periodically or for a sustained time, it is a sign of illness, stress, worry, or insecurity. Family and friends should encourage her to talk to them or to a doctor to explore her feelings and eating habits.

Many girls are always unhappy about their weight because they are trying to measure up to an image of the perfect woman. This image has been created in our society and is fostered by the media—advertisers, television, and magazines—as well as by the fashion, cosmetic, and film industries. These industries make a considerable profit by making people feel anxious and unattractive. The more anxious women and girls feel, the more money they will spend on products that they think will improve their appearance.

The image of the perfect body is everywhere, so it is not surprising that many girls are convinced that there is something wrong with them if they do not look like "her"—whoever is appearing on the cover of a slick, glossy magazine this month. Girls are led to believe that in order to be happy, popular, and successful, a girl must be a perfect size 7, have flawless skin, and possess just the right kind of hair and wardrobe to go with the perfect body. The perfect image for boys is less rigid, but they are also made to feel inadequate if they don't have clear skin, a muscular physique, and gorgeous hair.

The overemphasis on thinness in our society causes serious physical and emotional problems for girls. Worrying constantly about one's weight interferes with home, school, and social life. It is hard to concentrate on studying when you are preoccupied with thinking how miserable you feel about your body, or trying to ignore how hungry you feel while on a crash diet. It is no fun to anticipate going to a party or dance if you are convinced you look terrible. If these feelings persist, a girl can become withdrawn and depressed, and can overeat or go on extreme diets.

Fad diets, fasting, and extreme exercising can cause permanent damage to the body. Fad diets upset the digestive system. Excessive exercising can affect the menstrual cycle by reducing the number of fat cells which hold hormones needed for menstruation.

An obsession with being thin can lead to two life-threatening eating disorders. Many young women suffer from *bulimia*. A bulimic eats compulsively (binges) and then vomits or takes laxatives (purges). She routinely repeats this pattern because she is terrified of being overweight, even when she is not. *Anorexia* is a disease which is closely connected to body image and one's self-concept. An anorexic girl severely reduces her food intake or goes through cycles of binging and purging and fasting. Anorexics lose an extreme amount of weight and seem to develop a distorted body image, insisting they are fat when they are, in fact, dangerously emaciated.

Anorexia and bulimia can be treated and cured, especially if they are diagnosed early. Treatment includes therapy to help the girl understand that she is unhappy, and why she is trying to starve herself to death. She may be reacting to the expectations that she, her family, or society has set for the ideal woman; she may be trying to control her overwhelming feelings of inadequacy by not eating, thus eliminating womanly features such as curves and menstrual periods.

A girl who is worried about her weight needs to be reassured by friends that she is attractive the way she is. In fact, all friends need to offer each other encouragement to accept their bodies, and to enjoy their differences, rather than trying to look alike. If a friend is really overweight for her height and body frame, she should see a doctor or nurse practitioner who can help her develop a realistic and healthy diet and exercise plan. Most of all, she must examine *why* she is so worried. She might begin by asking herself, "Where did I get the idea there was something wrong with my body? Where did I get the image I am striving for?" Feeling good about your weight is an important aspect of a healthy self-image. Young men and women need to support and encourage images of females in the media as unique, independent, thinking individuals, and express their opposition to those money-making campaigns that have devastating negative effects on female self-image.

Skin

Almost everyone has some degree of acne during adolescence because of hormonal changes. Doctors and researchers have now found that the tendency towards acne is probably inherited, that diet is neither the cause nor the cure for acne, and that lack of cleanliness does not cause acne. Acne results when cells that line an oil duct to the skin's surface stick together and then block the opening, trapping the oil beneath the skin's surface. Everyone has oil glands (there are 15,000 to 20,000 in the face alone), and at puberty these oil glands start secreting more oil as a result of hormonal changes. Anything that triggers the production of more oil will cause a flare-up of acne. There is some connection between emotions and acne. When you are under stress or are very anxious, your adrenal glands work overtime to stimulate the formation of hormones. These hormones stimulate the production of oil and increase the chances of blemishes.

Most doctors recommend daily cleaning with a mild soap. Serious acne can be treated medically and you should seek professional help for stubborn acne, instead of being miserable.

Here's some advice girls have for boys:

Please don't:

☐ feel uncomfortable if we're taller than you.
☐ kid us about big or little breasts.
☐ make fun of our big feet.
☐ joke about "zits" (especially since we have that problem in common).

Please do:

☐ be considerate of your sister's privacy.
☐ be yourself.
☐ show respect for all girls.
☐ like us for what we are.

Boys: am I normal?

These are a few examples of physical traits that boys may feel insecure about:

"Am I the right height for my age?"
"Why am I the shortest in my class?"
"Will I always be short, or will I at least be average?"

"What is the normal penis size for boys my age?"
"Is my penis too small?"

"Why do I have so many blemishes?"
"Will girls think I look terrible?"
"How do you get rid of blemishes?"

"What's happening to me?"
"Does this happen to all the guys?"
"Is there something wrong with me?"

These are all normal insecurities that boys have as
they develop from boy to man. As their bodies change
they are concerned with what is normal and what is
abnormal.

Height

A boy first looks about and compares himself with
other boys his own age. If he sees that he is slightly
shorter than some and taller than others, he may not
be too concerned. However, if he is shorter than the
majority, he will be likely to see it as a problem and develop some insecure feelings about it. Society and the
media (television, movies, magazines) have promoted
the idea that short men are less manly. This is unfor-
tunate because it is not true, yet boys continue to
worry about being short. If a boy is taller than everyone else, this too can lead to insecurity. People make
the assumption that he must be interested in basketball since he is so tall—but they may be completely
wrong! He may be angry that people assume they

know his interests and talents, or want to channel them in a certain direction.

Family and friends are becoming more sensitive to how a boy feels about his height, yet adults may still make remarks that make him uncomfortable ("How's the air up there?"), and peers may still call him names like "shorty," "shrimp," or "midget." Tall or short, he may need to develop a standard retort for these comments. ("I was born this way. What's your excuse?")

Searching for explanations for a boy's height will not help, because explanations probably won't relieve his concern. Reading in books or pamphlets about puberty, growth patterns, and growth spurts may help lessen his anxiety. But although his size will continue to change throughout his adolescence, he will have to learn to live with it eventually.

Penis Size

This is a major concern of *all* male adolescents. The reason for this is that boys have been led to believe that, next to the brain and the heart, this is the most important organ a man has. It symbolizes his masculinity and he believes that a big penis means he's a "real man." Nothing could be farther from the truth. Penis size has nothing to do with the capacity to perform sexually or with fertility. But most boys do not know who to turn to for correct information. It is difficult to clear up the myths surrounding penis size and masculinity because it is an insecure feeling that almost all men in our society keep to themselves. This insecurity goes away as a male matures and finds out that size is not an important factor in being sexually attractive or having children.

Acne

Male adolescents are concerned with their appearance, and facial blemishes can be extremely upsetting. This is true for both sexes, especially with the message we get (via the media) that any flaw or imperfection will mean loneliness and heartache. Acne can interfere with dating and interacting with others. Like other physical changes during adolescence, acne has to run its course and usually clears up eventually. However, if a boy thinks that his skin problem is serious, he should see a doctor, because there are effective medical treatments for bad cases.

Nocturnal Emissions (Wet Dreams)

A wet dream is the informal name for what happens when a boy involuntarily ejaculates during sleep. It is extremely common and normal, and usually accompanies a dream about sex. It may happen frequently or only occasionally. Unfortunately, many boys have not been told that it is likely to happen. If a boy is not informed, or is misinformed about why and how wet dreams occur, he may think that it is weird, immoral, or sick. He may worry that there's something wrong with him. He doesn't want to ask questions or talk about it because of his own embarrassment or uncertainty. Boys generally have a hard time talking about their personal concerns with peers and others, so there may be little opportunity for parents, teachers, or friends to clarify what is going on. It is important for a boy to get information about the physical changes occurring in his body. He can get accurate information from books and pamphlets that explain the human body in general or, more specifically, puberty.

Social Development

Girls and boys: How do I get along with friends?

One way people have of overcoming insecurity and developing security is to be a part of a large or small group. People do not always consciously decide to join a group; often they find that they gradually became part of one. As an individual, you gain a sense of security by sharing the group's identity. Being a member of a group makes it easier to find answers to some questions: how to wear your hair, how to behave, what to wear, what to do for fun. The group may be a small circle of friends, three or four boys or girls. Within the group, you may have one special, close friend. The qualities of the relationships (all to each other or in the single, special friendship) are probably the same. Friendship means sharing and giving: trust, loyalty, understanding, comfort, and support go both ways.

Being a friend in any relationship brings responsibilities and rewards and helps each person overcome insecurity. In addition to groups and individual friends, some kids find a sense of security in belonging to an athletic team; a music, theater, or dance group; a ski club; the school newspaper; or a community volunteer organization. Of course, not everybody wants or needs to be part of a group. Instead, some may choose to have one special friend. When you are with this friend, you feel secure, comfortable, and confident—just as you do when you are with a group of good friends.

Time Together, Time Alone

As important as it is to have time with a friend or group of friends, it is also important to have and enjoy time alone. When you are alone, you relax, reflect on your life, and develop personal interests: reading, sewing, writing, constructing, painting. When you are alone, you have the chance to think about your securities and insecurities. Some people are afraid to be alone and get to know themselves. They busy themselves constantly with work, activities, other people, or television. If they would try solitude and use time alone for thinking and working through problems, they might not find it so scary.

Looking Back

☐ I just didn't want to be alone.

☐ I used to bug my mother all the time because all the girls had certain jeans and certain shoes: they only shopped in certain stores. I just wanted to be like everybody else.

☐ There was a bunch of guys I really wanted to be with. Finally I got in the group and before long I realized I didn't really like them.

☐ It was such a big deal. I mean if you wanted to be asked out by a certain boy, then you had to be in a certain group of girls.

☐ You had to be in a group or you would get stuck with other boys. Now that sounds mean. I guess it was.

Beginning Dating

Girls: How should I act?

Sunday Night

Dear Diary,

I have some things on my mind that I can't seem to talk with anyone about. There's this boy who I think likes me, and I really like him. I'm not sure if it's okay for me to ask him out or if I should wait for him to ask me out first. My friends think I should ask him, but my oldest sister says it's wrong for a girl to ask a boy. I don't know what to do. Maybe I'll figure it out tomorrow.

Monday Night

Dear Diary,

I think about Gary all day long! I think I should ask him because he seems kind of shy. The only problem is he's always with his friends, and I'm embarrassed. I don't know how to get him alone. And how should I

97

ask him? What should I say? What if he says "no"? I'll feel like such a jerk!

Tuesday Night

Dear Diary,

Well, I finally did it. I asked him to go out with me to the movies. And he said "yes." I thought all my problems were over, but now it seems like they've just begun. Should I tell my parents he asked me out? What will they think if they know I asked him? And now how will we get to the movies? Too much to think about. Good night.

Thursday Night

Dear Diary,

I decided to wear my new yellow shirt with my good jeans. I wish I knew a different way to fix my hair. I guess I'll just wear it down the ways I always do. I wonder if boys worry about what to wear! I was so excited and now I feel so scared. I wonder if other girls feel like this on a first date? I wonder if he'll try to kiss me? What if he doesn't??

Friday Night

Dear Diary,

Well, we went. It was fun, I guess, but I was so nervous. My mother dropped Carolyn and me off and his brother drove him and Randy. The movie was so stupid! And Carolyn and I spent so much time in the Girls' Room—he probably thinks I have some kind of problem or something! It was kind of fun part of the time but he'll probably never ask me out again. A disappointed good night.

Saturday Afternoon

Dear Diary,

Today has been the best day of my life ever! I went to the store for my mother and I met Gary up the street and he said, want to take a bike ride? We just rode our bikes all over the place and talked and talked. And, guess what, he was worried about all the same things I was. He was wondering how he could talk to me alone, away from my friends. He was worried about what to say. He was really worried that I'd say no when he first asked me for a date. He wasn't sure whether or not to tell his parents a girl asked him out! We have so much in common.

Going out on your first date may be scary. You may feel anxious and jittery about accepting an invitation, or while you are on the date, or when you think about it afterward. Suddenly you have no appetite, or your mouth is dry and your hands are sweaty. This is completely normal. Even as you gain more experience relating to boys, you may still feel nervous each time you go out, depending on where you are going and who the boy is. Double dating can sometimes help you overcome your shyness, as there will be less pressure on you to keep up a lively conversation. Above all, try to act naturally. Behave as you would with any other friend. And remember, he is probably just as nervous as you are!

Boys: How should I act?

There have been lots of changes in the dating behaviors of young men. First, boys today are not dating as early as their older brothers and fathers did. There is now group dating, where a group of boys will meet a group of girls and each person pays for himself or herself. There are certain occasions where it's necessary to date singly, such as a school dance, the prom, or a birthday party. For these occasions, in addition to the traditional ritual of boys asking girls out, it is much more acceptable today than it used to be for girls to ask boys out. If a girl does ask a boy out, however, many traditional parents who are unaccustomed to

the new roles and rules may react with disapproval—
perhaps with a long pause, followed by the comment,
"Nice girls don't ask boys out." Nevertheless, boys
should not feel odd or guilty about accepting a girl's
invitation.

For a boy, the biggest source of insecurity about dating is the possibility of being rejected, which would
reinforce any negative thoughts he has about himself.
It's true that a girl may not want to go out with anyone
she does not feel attracted to. On the other hand, it is
very likely that her excuse is real—she may actually be
busy that night, or her parents may really have said
she could not go out. Whatever the reason, being rejected is part of growing up. Both sexes have to learn
to handle it.

Other insecurities that boys may have about dating
may sound like worries, and they are. A boy is bound
to be worried about his self-image, his ability to carry
on a conversation, what she thinks of him. Some of
the questions he will ask himself before he asks her
out are: Does she like me? Will she think I'm a good
dancer? Will she let me kiss her? Will she like how I
dress?

Girls should not assume that boys are interested
only in "making out" or physical relationships. Most
boys want the same things that girls do—warmth, a
sense of caring, and someone with whom to share feelings and experiences. Boys may tend to talk among
themselves more about the physical side of relationships, but that often happens because they are not
used to sharing their feelings as openly as girls.

Self-image

Girls and boys: Who am I? Where do I fit in?

Self-image refers to your image or mental picture of
yourself. When you consider self-image, you confront

your honest feelings about yourself. Your self-image includes your feelings about your appearance, your personality, and your intellect; and about your relationships within your family, with other adults in your life, and with your friends. As you take an honest look at yourself, you confront basic securities and insecurities. You know what you feel good about and what feels bad. Feeling very bad about just one thing about yourself can affect how you feel about everything.

If you know somebody who is behaving in a difficult way, or who seems very unhappy, or who is extremely overweight or underweight, there is usually a reason. The reason may be a hidden insecurity. She may think she is not smart enough, or he may feel he is not loved and wanted by his family. You cannot solve the problem for another person, but you can try to understand, and you can show that you care and that you can listen. This may mean that you have to be very tolerant and accepting of someone's behavior, so you will have to learn to be patient and understanding. The most important thing that you can do is to demonstrate that you are a friend, that you like the person. You can help point out his or her positive qualities and strengths. For instance, you might encourage a girl who feels insecure because she is short to develop a style of dress that is unique and interesting. You might lend support to a boy who feels insecure about his ability in sports by helping him work extra hard to develop his science skills. If a person can begin to feel good about him- or herself in one way, he or she may gradually overcome the source of insecurity.

Family Relationships

Boys and girls

All families have some problems at one time or another. If your family is having problems, you may be feeling very insecure and very much alone. You may be uneasy about what is happening; but if it is a temporary problem and parents and siblings resolve it, your worrying will end.

If you are in a family where there are basic problems over a long period of time, this can lead to insecurities which are difficult to overcome. You may wonder: Is everybody's family like this? Why can't I have a "normal" family?

Here is a list of some serious family problems that can be the source of kids' insecurities:

Serious illness. If a parent or sibling is seriously ill, you may feel insecure because you and your family cannot do some of the things other families do, such as picnics, vacations, and spontaneous outings. Perhaps also you fear losing that family member and don't know how you could handle your grief.

Alcoholism. If a parent has an alcohol problem, kids may feel insecure because they can't rely on that parent and can't tell others about it. There may be a lot of tension between parents.

Emotional and physical abuse. A kid can feel as if he or she is making an abusive parent angry. It is very important not to feel guilty and to get professional help (at school, at a hospital, at a police station, or from an adult you can trust). It is the parent who abuses who has a problem and needs treatment: you need to report the problem so you can protect yourself.

A parent's unemployment. Kids may feel they have to do something to relieve financial stress. That may or may not be appropriate.

In a family other things can happen that can make you feel insecure. Usually these things are circumstances that kids in the family cannot control, such as moving, parents having a legal dispute, or a sister or brother getting into some kind of trouble. Somehow, kids may think they have caused the problem or kids may imagine that it is their fault if they cannot solve the problem. But kids cannot be responsible for their parents' problems.

Understanding Friends

Boys and girls

Family relationships form the basis for relationships outside the family. You may have heard of something called *basic trust*. Basic trust is developed early in life between parent and child. If this first relationship is good, a person will find it easy to have good relationships later. Sometimes kids do not develop basic trust because their parents have too many problems. This can make it difficult for kids to make friends and get along with teachers, coaches, and other adults. This may all sound like "shrink talk," but even you can become a bit of a psychologist and try to figure out what is making a friend unhappy or insecure.

If you have a friend who has a serious home problem, you might suggest they talk to a teacher, counselor, the school social worker, or some other adult they can trust. This part is difficult, both because your friend may have a hard time trusting anyone, and because it may not be easy for you to make this suggestion. It helps if you reassure the friend that everybody has problems and feelings they need to talk about and share. If there is no one in the family your friend can talk to, then he or she needs to find somebody outside the family who will keep the information confidential.

Here is a list of problems and dilemmas that all families experience:

Parents and Extended Family

☐ Disagreements and minor arguments: Who should cook? Who should mow the lawn? Whose fault is it the car broke down?

□ Periods of indecision: When should we take our family vacation? Where will we go for Thanksgiving dinner?

□ Housing for an elderly person: What can we afford? When should they move? Will they be happy?

Sisters and Brothers

□ Bugging: Why don't you play with me?

□ Aggravation: Why is your music so loud?

□ Jealousy: How come he got a new bike and I didn't?

Remember that it is normal (once in a while) to imagine that everybody else's family is happier, or more "normal," or more content or peaceful than your own. It is normal (once in a while) to imagine how much happier you would be in a different family. No one has a *perfect* family.

Performance

Boys and girls: Am I good enough? Am I smart enough?

Situation

Sharon is taking Spanish this year. She does all the homework assignments and tries to practice the words out loud when she is home alone. But in school, she gets so nervous when the teacher calls on her that she can barely talk. Frequently, she wants to ask a question, but she has to ask in Spanish, and she is afraid to try.

Sharon is not alone! She must remember the subject is new for everybody. She may be worried about the opinions of other kids; but if another student is critical or thinks it is funny when someone makes an error, he or she may be the one who is more insecure. If Sharon can be brave and speak up, she will learn faster, enjoy it more, and help other kids who are feeling the same way.

Situation

Dave is his soccer team's best scorer. Near the end of the game the score is tied when an opponent commits a foul. Dave's team is awarded a penalty kick, and he has to kick it. If he scores, the team wins; if he misses his team will only tie.

First of all, Dave should relax. His teammates can identify with how tense he must feel. You have heard of the power of positive thinking. Try it! Another way to say it is "visualization." Dave might visualize or picture himself relaxed and alone, making a perfect kick; tune everything else out of his mind; take a few deep breaths; and proceed. He should also remember that family and friends will know he has done his best.

Situation

Kristin has been taking flute lessons for two years. Her music teacher thinks that she is ready to perform alone in a concert. She is very anxious about doing this.

If her teacher believes that Kristin is ready, Kristin should trust her judgment. The teacher would not encourage Kristin if she did not believe that Kristin could handle the challenge. Kristin could ask her music teacher or a friend for tips on how to prepare to perform. For instance, some performers focus their eyes on one point (such as a window or an exit sign), concentrate on it, and if they feel anxious when they look at the audience, they return their eyes to that object. Their concentration helps overcome their nervousness.

Situation

John is staying overnight at a friend's. His friend's mother asks him to set the table for dinner. John never has to set the table at his own house and he is not sure how to do it.

▬▬▬

John is worried that if he sets the table incorrectly, he will be criticized by his friend's mother. There is nothing wrong with admitting that he is not sure what to do and asking her for advice. If he does decide to do it his own way (which could be a creative, problem-solving adventure!), he can prepare to watch her reaction in a positive manner. If she suggests changes, she is not criticizing him as a person, but simply the act of table-setting.

This chapter has explored many dimensions of insecurity—from insecurities about physical growth and development to insecurities about performance in school, at home, and socially. The big question remains, "Will my friends and I ever grow out of this?" Yes, mostly! Keep in mind that no individual is ever completely free of some insecurity about something, but as we grow we learn to adapt and accept our own strengths and weaknesses.

Anger

Dear Beth,

My parents tell me what to do *all the time.* It makes me so mad I want to scream. They tell me when to get up and what to wear and what time to come home. Last night Mother said, "Don't forget to brush your teeth," and I just yelled "I won't!" and slammed the door. Sometimes I think all they care about is that I get good marks and keep clean. I'm fourteen. Am I an ungrateful daughter?

Screaming Fits

■

Dear Screaming Fits,

No, you are a normal teenager, and probably a very nice one. Kids your age need to grow up and gain more independence from their parents. You want to run more of your own life, and you resent being treated as if you were still a little child.

Some kids use anger as a way to put distance between themselves and their parents. They believe this hastens their independence by forcing more separation. Some kids get angry because it is actually scary to contemplate being totally on their own, and fear often gets turned into anger.

What you need to do is work out your differences with your parents in a more mature way. Slamming and yelling are good releases for your emotions, but do not accomplish what you want because they make you seem even more childish to your parents. Talk to them instead. Say, "It makes me feel helpless when you keep nagging me this way. I feel you think I'm a baby. Can't we figure out some better ways for you to give me more chances to run my own life?"

The emotion of anger is not bad, but an important

part of adolescent adjustment is to learn to use it in a more mature way.

Beth

■

Dear Beth,

Our gym teacher gets on my case all the time. He thinks I'm lazy, just because I'm not as good as some of the other guys. For a while I tried extra hard, but he kept on being sarcastic, so I gave it up. What's the use? But he gets me so mad I feel like I may explode. I keep it all inside me, but I dream about punching his big nose. Once I got nerve enough to ask him why he didn't pick on someone else for a change, but he just smiled and made more of his little remarks.

Tim

■

Dear Tim,

It is infuriating to be picked on unfairly, and it sounds like you have a good reason to be angry. You've got two problems: how to cope with the anger, and how to cope with the situation that is making you so mad.

Expressing anger is hard for most people. Little boys just hit out when they get mad, but their parents soon teach them to use words, not fists. Some grown men still resort to blows, but we expect "civilized" people to talk out their anger instead. So you are wise not to punch, especially a teacher, which would only get you in trouble. But you must talk to someone about your feelings, otherwise the anger will seethe inside you, and then burst out later in some inappropriate way, such as cursing out your mother, or beating up on your little brother.

Try to cure the problem by talking once more with the gym teacher. Tell him you really are not a lazy person, and ask him to tell you ways you can prove this to him. Most teachers are reasonable when a problem is brought to their attention in a reasonable way.

If this fails, go to your parents or the school authorities to protest the unfair treatment. This teacher should not be sarcastic with any student. Use your anger to try to make constructive changes.

Beth

Here are some powerful words for this strong emotion: anger, wrath, frustration, rage, fury, aggravation, temper, madness.

Anger is often a disguise or a mask for other emotions. And often other emotions disguise or mask anger. We will be exploring why it is so hard to show our true feelings, especially when we are feeling a mixture of emotions.

Younger boys and girls are sometimes taught to deal differently with anger. In the past, it was considered inappropriate for girls to display anger, so girls were taught to suppress or hide their anger: to be passive, sweet, and nice. If a girl has been taught by her parents, grandparents, and teachers to suppress her anger, she will have trouble recognizing the source of her anger when she is older. She may know she's upset, but may not know that it is anger she is feeling. Or, if she knows she's angry, she may not know why. She has practiced behaving calm and cheerful for so long that it may be hard for her to identify and express her feelings. Girls need to learn that it is okay to feel angry and express it effectively.

Often girls say they are angry when, in fact, they are really feeling hurt; or sometimes they'll say they feel hurt when they are feeling angry. Here are some examples of situations that cause anger in girls:

☐ Another girl flirts with a boy I'm going out with or she gets next to him in line (anger, jealousy, worry).
☐ People think I'm younger than I am and call me "shorty" (anger and insecurity).
☐ My brother shows off in front of my friends by walking around and singing and dancing (anger, aggravation, embarrassment).
☐ My mother says, "How come you didn't bring any books home?" and I say, "I don't have any homework" and she bugs me anyway (anger and aggravation).
☐ The gym teacher doesn't believe me when I say I'm

sick and she makes me put on my gym clothes anyway (anger and frustration).
□ Friends make fun of my sister, or make comments
about the kids she hangs around with, or say things
like "How can you stand your sister?" (Anger, humiliation, pride.)
□ I see a pair of pants I like and they don't come in my
size (anger and disappointment).
□ I can't get my locker combination to work! (Anger
and frustration.)
□ My brother yells at my grandmother, and she gets
upset (anger and compassion).
□ My bike was stolen—I'll never forget how angry I was
(anger, hurt, powerlessness).
□ My grandfather asks me a question and I answer
and then he keeps asking more and more questions
(anger and aggravation).
□ I get mad when I forget what I was going to say
(frustration).
□ My mother folds my brother's laundry and not mine
(anger and outrage).

As a boy grows up he is often allowed, even encouraged, to express his anger verbally and physically.
Physical expression of anger (kicking a tire or punching a pillow) is all right if no one is hurt. Although it
is good to get anger out, it is also important for boys
to examine the source of their anger. Some boys are
not taught how to discuss their feelings. So, following
an angry outburst, they may feel better briefly but a
vague feeling of confusion may linger. Boys must understand how their behavior affects those around
them, and where their feelings are coming from.
For boys, anger often masks fear. A boy may be
scared he won't measure up to a task, or that he'll be
embarrassed or humiliated. Sometimes boys turn hurt
feelings into angry feelings because they have been
taught that it is okay to show anger—but not fear or

sensitivity. A boy is supposed to act tough or brave, not hurt or sad. When a boy acts angry, he may be feeling frightened or hurt underneath. A boy is more likely to say, "John really ticked me off when he left without me" rather than admit, "My feelings were hurt when John went on ahead without me." He may say, "Dan is crazy if he thinks I'm going to help the Girl Scouts build theater sets" rather than, "I'm worried about what the guys will say if I help the girls." He'll mask his nervousness with an angry, tough tone.

Parents, teachers, adults, and other friends must encourage boys to be more honest about all their feelings. One way is to compliment a boy when he is open about his feelings. Let him know clearly that you appreciate his honesty or sensitivity with comments like: "Jed, I really admired the way you went and explained to Mr. Blake why you were angry about the concert being cancelled."

Here are some typical situations in which *boys* feel angry:

☐ My mother wants me to clean the yard and I want to get out on my boat (aggravation and anger).

☐ I work really hard on a project and the teacher gives me a low grade (frustration and anger).

☐ I'm working making something and it's going great and then I do one stupid thing and wreck it (frustration and anger).

☐ A referee calls me out of the game for fouling (humiliation and anger).

☐ I can't get my bicycle to work (frustration and anger).

☐ My sister borrows money and won't pay me back (irritation and anger).

☐ My father gives me lectures and tells me what I should be interested in—like politics (aggravation and anger).

☐ I make plans to go camping with the guys and then

my mother says I can't go (disappointment and anger).
- □ My brother beats me up for no reason at all (anger and confusion).
- □ I make a deal with my parents and they won't keep their part. Like going halves for a new bike—I earned my share of the money and they said they weren't going to pay for the rest after all (anger and disappointment).
- □ I build something outside in the yard and somebody comes and wrecks it (anger and hurt).

Learning to express anger appropriately is important. You need to understand where your angry feeling is coming from in order to learn what to do with it. If you're feeling mad, try asking yourself:

- □ Who am I angry at?
- □ What did they do or say to make me angry? Is it what they said or how they said it that made me angry?
- □ Are my feelings hurt? If so, why?
- □ Am I afraid of something?
- □ Are there any other feelings mixed with the anger? What are they?

Recognizing the source of anger is difficult for several reasons. Anger may be mixed with other emotions. Often it seems to appear suddenly. Since you may be so busy in the midst of the feeling, it can be hard to stop and think clearly. Anger can be so strong, it can be frightening to imagine what you might do with it.

Expressing anger appropriately

There are many ways of expressing anger. Some people (more frequently girls) respond to anger by crying or withdrawing into silence. Others (more frequently boys) slam doors and act aggressively—vandalizing, bullying others, and being physically abusive. Still others may brood or take out their anger on people or things not directly responsible.

Your family's example and teaching help shape how you behave when you are angry. Parents may disagree about how daughters and sons should express their anger. Parents' ideas about how you should behave are often reinforced by neighbors and others in your community. Some parents allow kids to display and discuss their anger; others discourage such discussions. Some adults continue to treat boys and girls differently, with traditional expectations and different standards. Girls are allowed to cry openly; boys are not. Boys are allowed to raise their voices; girls are not. School also has an influence on how you express your anger. Some schools and teachers encourage students to discuss positive and negative emotions; others do not. Even television affects your behavior. Some shows reinforce traditional values and behaviors in shows with quiet females always trying to please powerful, aggressive males; others reflect some of the changing attitudes in shows with strong, assertive women and sensitive, gentle men. The way you express your anger is a product of all these familial and societal influences. The confusion about how to express your anger, however, is a result of the shift away from clearly defined, traditional roles for men and women.

Here are some phrases that people use to describe being angry:

blow a fuse	ticked off
blow one's cool	do a slow burn
blow one's stack	have a short fuse
blow one's top	blind with rage
blow up	lose your head
hit the ceiling	
see red	

Keep in mind that displaying some anger is normal and very human. Mental-health professionals would be concerned about a person who never displayed anger.

It is important to realize that there are acceptable (constructive) and unacceptable (destructive) ways of expressing or dealing with one's anger. Banging doors, yelling, and throwing things are usually not considered constructive and only make one feel better for a minute or so. Crying can be a healthy release, but usually needs to be followed by some kind of action that resolves the situation. Clearly, violent aggression involving people or property is destructive and therefore undesirable.

The following methods can be used as a basis for working through anger. Each can be used constructively or destructively. You will bring your own strengths and weaknesses to each method.

Confrontation

This means that you tell the person directly that you are angry with him or her and explain why you are angry. Often this includes standing in front of them, looking them in the eye, and saying plainly that you are mad at them. Then you explain the reasons for your anger.

This method is usually effective and best tolerated with your siblings or peer group. It is more difficult with authority figures; they have more power than you do and, in the end, you often lose. For example, confronting a teacher or police officer can be risky, and it is likely to make them angrier. However, you can learn to confront your parents in a manner they can accept, so they can really hear what you're trying to say.

Internalization

This means keeping your anger inside. Internalization can be a useful way of coping with a minor aggravation or frustration rather than a major anger. Sometimes it is wise to internalize anger over small issues that are not worth arguing about. If it is truly a minor concern ("I can't stand the way my shoelace keeps breaking"), the momentary anger may pass. Unfortunately, internalization is strictly a short-term solution. Your anger will almost always come out, and be directed inappropriately at the wrong people, or make you physically ill with headaches, stomach aches, or sleeplessness. Only you can decide what issues or situations can be safely dealt with by internalizing anger.

Misdirection

This means focusing your behavior and feelings on something or someone who is not directly responsible for whatever is making you angry. This is destructive if your behavior hurts another person (who has nothing to do with the cause of your anger), or if you damage or destroy property. It can be constructive only if you are able to rechannel or redirect your angry energy into a more productive activity. For instance, if you are very angry with your grandmother but know you cannot confront her or resolve the issue, you may have to redirect your anger. Instead of venting your rage by hurting someone else's feelings or destroying that poster you never liked in your sister's room, use the energy in some vigorous activity (a fierce game of tennis or ping-pong) or do a job you will later be glad to have behind you (clean out your desk or notebook).

Handling anger

Here are two situations, one involving a boy and his brother, the other a mother and daughter. Three methods of coping with anger are explored.

1. It is Saturday morning and Jason is getting ready to meet his friends for a trip to the beach.

OLDER BROTHER   Jason, this is the last time I am going to ask you to clean up the mess you made in our room.

JASON   Yeah, yeah.

OLDER BROTHER   I think you'd better do it *right now*.

Jason is beginning to get angry. He can use confrontation, misdirection, or internalization to cope with his feelings.

Confrontation

JASON   (mumbles) Right now, right now.

OLDER BROTHER   What did you say?

JASON   Nothing. (He responds angrily because he knows he's going to be late.) I know I have to clean it up but I'm late to meet the guys. It really makes me mad that you say I have to do it right now. I promise I'll do it later.

OLDER BROTHER   Okay, but it really needs to be done now, because I won't be able to study until you clear away your things. I'll help you so you can get to the beach on time. But next week you'll have to help me with the yardwork.

In this case, confronting worked. Jason explained that he was willing to do the work (the basic issue), but that being told to "do it right now" made him angry and that he was concerned about missing his friends. His brother understood him and accepted a compromise.

Internalization

Jason remains silent, stomps off to the room, throws his clothes into the hamper, and shoves the rest of his mess in drawers and closets. His brother is satisfied because the task has been accomplished, but Jason goes to the beach with a headache because he has not verbalized his feelings. He is still upset because he is late meeting his friends and feels angry that his brother spoke to him in such a bossy manner.

Misdirection

Jason is still angry because he is late meeting his buddies. He is also angry because he is afraid to tell the guys what happened for fear they will laugh at him. So he makes up a flimsy excuse. As he is getting on the bus, he drops one coin into the box and accidentally misses with the other. The bus driver says, "Pick it up." Jason reacts angrily, "Pick it up yourself." The bus driver mumbles and Jason can make out the word "punk." Jason has now misdirected his anger at the bus driver. This is an unfair and unacceptable response to the situation.

2. It is Saturday afternoon and Joyce is planning to go downtown shopping at the mall.

JOYCE I'm going to catch the 1:00 bus to the mall, Mom.

MOTHER Fine. I just hope that Carol isn't going with you.

JOYCE But Mom, you know Carol is my best friend.

MOTHER I don't care. I don't want you to be with her.

The anger is beginning.

Confrontation

JOYCE But Mom, she's my friend. You're not being fair.

MOTHER You know that I don't trust her.

JOYCE But you can. Why are you so suspicious all the time, just because she got into trouble once? You don't understand. Anyway, I don't care what you think. She's my friend and I'm going with her.

The confrontation is in full force. Joyce is being honest and forthright about her anger, but if she continues in this vein she will only make her mother more stubborn.

As mentioned earlier, confrontation is difficult with authority figures such as parents and teachers. But if you can learn to confront in a caring and thoughtful manner, you can learn to work through your anger and find solutions.

Although her mother may have reason to be concerned about Carol's past behavior, Joyce believes her friend has changed. If Joyce yells and screams, this confrontation is likely to end in a no-win situation. But if Joyce could use a less heightened or angry tone of voice, she might be able to make her mother understand why she feels she can now trust Carol. She might suggest inviting Carol over for dinner so her mom can get to know her better. If Joyce can be calm and reasonable, she will be able to think, talk, and possibly negotiate a solution. She will use confrontation effectively.

Internalization

JOYCE All right, I'll just go with Susan. (Secretly she knows she'll meet Carol downtown.)

MOTHER Good.

JOYCE (To herself) Yeah, good for you, you mean. (Her body tightens with silent anger.)

Here Joyce has kept her anger inside and avoided a discussion or confrontation over the situation. But now she may be faced with a greater problem. Physically, she is aware that she does not feel good about what she has done. She will continue to feel guilty about sneaking out with her friend and will also still feel angry toward her mother.

Misdirection

JOYCE Yeah, Mom, I hear you. (To her little sister) Get out of my room, you little brat!
MOTHER What did you say?
JOYCE Nothing, Mom. (To her sister) And get your stupid clothes off my bed!

Instead of expressing her anger towards her mother, Joyce is taking it out on her little sister. This reaction is dangerous because the issue with her mother is left unresolved; she's damaging her relationship with her sister (especially if this happens all the time); her sister gets confused; and Joyce is still angry.

Learning to be assertive in order to express anger

Being assertive means feeling clear about your goals and how to achieve them. Learning how to say "no" is part of learning to assert yourself. So is learning to express anger in a constructive and acceptable manner.

Girls are learning to be more assertive—to express their opinions and their ideas more forcefully—in many ways. Traditionally, boys have demonstrated their anger more openly than girls; now girls are more free to express anger.

Girls coping with boys' anger

Brothers

As adolescents, brothers and sisters may often find themselves in conflict. You may argue about unequal chores, favored treatment from one parent or the other, or using each other's possessions. However, if

119

your brother's behavior is unacceptable to you, you often have your parents as allies in reprimanding him. So you may feel more able to express that anger.

If you borrow one of your brother's records without asking him, he may be angry with you. You may be willing to discuss what you did wrong (and even apologize), while he may not be willing to hear you; he may act out by yelling at you or breaking something of yours. You will have to wait until he calms down. You might try writing him a note and apologizing, or offering to do him a favor.

Sometimes a brother may be acting angry at you for no apparent reason. He may be angry because of a poor test grade he received or because the play he's in at school isn't going well. If your brother is angry and is misdirecting his anger at you, you should attempt to ignore it or get out of the same room for a while. If he gets aggressive when he is angry, you should tell your parents. If he gets away with aggressive behavior, it can become his way of expressing his anger as an adult, and eventually he may get into trouble or hurt someone. By telling your parents, you are helping him to realize that his behavior is unacceptable. To make yourself feel more comfortable about this method of handling the problem, you should warn him: "Listen, John, if you touch me, I'll tell Mom and Dad. I don't take that kind of treatment from anyone."

Girls who have brothers should take the opportunity to learn about boys from their siblings; since many other boys they know may act the same way, they'll be better able to understand them.

Conflicts between brothers and sisters are normal, and can usually be resolved without parental involvement.

Boys Who Are Friends

Boys get angry when they feel rejected, or if they feel that someone has made a fool of them. Being humiliated in front of his peers ("Your mother and I think you're too young to see that show") is likely to make a boy furious. Being called names that question their masculinity or physical ability ("sissy," "mama's boy," "shorty") or being subjected to jokes about their appearance (about having acne or clumsy big feet) or competing and losing (especially to a girl) are common situations that make boys angry.

When a friend is angry you can usually comfort him by being understanding. For instance, if he is angry because his parents won't let him go to a certain movie, you could say, "Parents are just weird sometimes. You'll get to go next time." Be careful not to let the understanding and comfort you give be misunderstood as romantic interest. Make sure he understands that you are being just a friend. He does not need rejection at this time. Boys and girls should also learn to respect each other's wishes. You might encourage him to express his feelings, but if he says, "I don't want to talk about it," don't bug him or nag him to talk. When he is ready, he will probably explain the problem.

Boyfriends

If a boyfriend is angry, be sure he is not misdirecting his anger at you because a parent or a teacher or a sibling has scolded him. If he frequently is abrupt with you for no apparent reason, or if he never seems to be in a happy or fun mood, he may be feeling angry. Even if you don't know why he's angry (and suspect he may be unable to figure out why), it's not good for him to take it out on you. If you find that he is doing this, don't let him! Tell him he isn't being fair and that his anger is damaging your relationship. Unresolved anger—yours or his—can be destructive. It can mount up and explode in a mean confrontation. Encourage your boyfriend to talk about his feelings by telling him that it is better to talk it out now, because otherwise the resentment and misunderstandings can build to the point where they destroy a relationship.

If special friends can communicate or confront each

other with caring when they get angry, they learn a very important skill that can be used in other relationships as well. If a boy is very angry about a larger issue (for example, he thinks you like his friend better than him, or he thinks your parents are too strict and unfair) and does not want to or can't talk about it openly and honestly, you might suggest a cooling-off period when you don't see each other. During that period, you'll have time and space to think. Be sure to tell him that you are not rejecting him, and that the time apart can give you both an opportunity to resolve the anger.

It is best to be honest and straightforward with each other, even with difficult emotions. On the other hand, there may be times when your boyfriend is angry at someone or something else, or at you, and you can't figure out why. If you don't feel it's endangering all the trust and affection you have for him, or if the

relationship is important enough for you to endure a stormy period, you may just have to live with it.

Boys coping with girls' anger

Sisters

When a girl is feeling angry, she may be in her room pounding her pillow on the bed, she may be crying, or she may be in a terribly bad mood and quick-tempered with you. When you know your sister is feeling angry, encourage her to talk about what is bothering her. If she is angry at one or both of your parents, you may be able to sympathize with her and let her express her rage. When she calms down, you can examine the problem together. If you think she is in the wrong or her anger at them is unfair, you can perhaps help her see the situation more objectively. If you think she is right and her anger is justified, you can commiserate (join in her feeling of anger) with her. Whether or not you think her anger is justified, she is *feeling* it and must *express* it.

Girls Who Are Friends

If you have a friend who is angry, she may want to talk on and on, about the person or situations that made her mad. Some of what she says may sound irrational and unreasonable, but let her go on for a while. She needs to get it out. As a friend, let her know verbally or nonverbally that you'll keep confidential any crazy or silly things she may say when she is angry. You might suggest an activity such as a long walk or a bike ride to reduce her tension and get rid of excess energy. When she is calmer, try to brainstorm solutions to her dilemma; this will help her deal constructively with her anger. If she is angry at a teacher, a letter or a request for a conference with the teacher may work. If she is mad at herself (for example, for failing a test),

123

help her not to be so hard on herself. "You'll do better next time"; "Everybody has a bad day once in a while and teachers know that too"; "Your life does not depend on *one* test grade"; "Maybe you can take it over" are some of the things you might say to her.

Girlfriends

When a girl is angry at something her boyfriend has done, she may pout, withdraw, insist that nothing is wrong—anything but show the depth of her anger. She may minimize the angry feeling, saying things like "Oh, I guess I just expected too much and my feelings were just hurt when you forgot my birthday, that's all," rather than "I was furious all day because I knew you had forgotten my birthday." Try to develop a relationship where she can feel comfortable examining her true feelings and experiencing them. Let her know that you are strong enough to hear the truth and that you know it will improve your relationship if you both learn to share and communicate better.

Some girls have no problem at all showing their anger! This is generally healthy and good. Of course, if she is angry *all* the time she is with you—at something at home or school, something that has nothing to do with you—anger may be a serious problem for her. You can let her know that you feel she is misdirecting her anger and that you will not take it. She must discover the hidden source of her anger and deal with it directly.

Acceptable ways of dealing with anger

Here are some practical suggestions for coping with anger:

1. If you are in conflict and feel angry toward an authority figure, ask the person to be democratic and give you five minutes of uninterrupted time to ex-

plain your side. (This does not work all the time because not all adults operate democratically.)

2. Be a good listener and try to get all the facts. After all, that is what you are expecting from the other person. Then try to determine whether or not your anger is justified.

3. Avoid letting your emotions rule your behavior. Think first and act later. Some people find it useful to count to ten before saying anything.

4. Request a cooling-off period to think about the cause of the anger.

5. Sort out other emotions mixed with your anger—especially hurt, insecurity, and fear.

6. If you cannot resolve a problem, think about asking a neutral third party to evaluate the situation.

7. If you feel like getting violent, use a punching bag. (Hitting the wall is counterproductive; you will find

125

that the conflict is over long before your hand heals.)

8. If you are aggravated or frustrated over small things, try not to take it out on others. Just try to handle it alone. Silent simmering or cursing may be all you can do. Physical exercise (a quick jog) may help.

Helplessness

Dear Beth,

These two big kids at my school are making my life hell. When I come by they call me "fatso" and "fag," and get all the other kids to do it, too. They grab my books and throw them around. Sometimes they even take my money. I can't fight both of them! I told my teacher, but he just said to ignore them. I asked my mom if I could change schools, but she said, "You have to learn to get along in this world." I've tried being friendly. I tried avoiding them. Nothing works.

Scapegoat

Dear Scapegoat,

It is terrible being at the mercy of bigger guys like this, and it certainly doesn't improve your confidence. Your teacher is right that these two fellows won't get a kick out of calling names if they can't get a rise out of you, so if you can possibly pull it off, try not responding to them.

A more likely strategy is to respond with humor. If you learn to pass it off with a funny remark or joke, you can get the other kids laughing *with* you, instead of *at* you.

Also try to have friends stick with you as much as possible, so you won't be outnumbered when these two boys are around.

Remember, tough as this is, the people who have the real problem are the bullies—you are minding your own business, while they are acting badly. So, even though they put you in a helpless position sometimes, don't let what they say affect your opinion of yourself.

127

People who have to bully and domineer others are the ones with the real character faults.

Beth

■

Dear Beth,

My parents treat me like a baby! I'm thirteen years old, and I have to be in bed by 9:00. I can't hang around with my friends after school. "You won't get anything accomplished," my mom says. When I try to explain that I won't have any friends left, she just doesn't seem to care. When I wanted to tell her about a boy I liked, she yelled at me, "I don't want to hear about it." How can I grow up if she doesn't let me?

Annie C.

■

Dear Annie C.,

I get lots of letters from girls (and boys) who feel that their parents treat them unfairly. Try to understand that all parents worry, and often with good reason. Perhaps you could begin by asking your mother to consider letting you go to a particular event (a school dance, a swim at the community pool) and make arrangements to be home by, say, 10:00 p.m. By coming home on time and safely, perhaps you can help her understand that you don't just want to hang out every night, but you want to begin to gain some independence and demonstrate that you can be responsible.

Parents may also worry that you'll get into trouble or be negatively influenced by friends. Maybe you can share with your mother some of the things you and your girl friends talk about when you're together (school concerns, clothes, dreams, boys); it may help her to have a better idea of what's on your mind and on your friends' minds.

The issue with boys is difficult. Your mother may think that because you like a boy, you'll be less close to her and the family. Of course, this doesn't have to be, but it may have been that way for her when she was young. Sometimes a grandmother, aunt, or friend of the family may be able to help you and your mother to understand each other and to communicate better.

Beth

Scapegoat and Annie C. are both experiencing feelings of helplessness. They are faced with daily problems over which they feel they have no control. They have tried to find solutions and they have asked for advice. Nothing has worked and each continues to feel helpless.

Everyone experiences feelings of helplessness occasionally. It is important to understand the feeling because it can be like a snowball. It starts with a small feeling over a particular event, but the feelings get bigger and bigger as it rolls along—so big that you end up feeling helpless all the time and do not know why. It is important to realize that sometimes we attempt to solve a problem and our solution does not work. This happens occasionally, and we must learn to accept that we cannot solve all the problems all the time.

Where does this feeling of helplessness come from? It can come from events at home, in the neighborhood, and at school; and, more and more today, from events in distant cities and countries. Every day we hear about so many events that it is impossible to stop and examine how we feel about each one. How do you sort out those events over which you have control, those you may control sometimes, those over which you will gain control as you get older, and those over which you have no control? Consider the following situations and try to think what your responses might be to each one. As you read, you can ask yourself the following questions:

☐ What can I do about the problem?
☐ Will this solve the problem?
☐ If I cannot solve the problem, can I do something that will make me feel better?
☐ What if I try to solve the problem and what I try does not work? How will I feel?
☐ How will I feel if there is absolutely nothing I can do about the situation?

The situations in which kids experience helplessness are the same for girls and boys. Here are several. Some possible solutions are discussed under "Finding Solutions and Accepting Realities," below.

1. You went on a trip with your friends and lost your money; they cannot help you out because they have just enough money for themselves.
2. Your friend's parents are getting a divorce and your friend feels guilty and wonders if it is her fault.
3. One of your teachers shouts at the class all day.
4. Your room is a mess.
5. A nuclear power plant is opening in your state.
6. You just saw a television special about children starving in India.
7. You do not have the money to buy your mother a birthday present.
8. You read in the newspaper about an earthquake in Italy that leaves hundreds without food, clothing, or shelter.
9. The people next door have a dog that they do not treat well.
10. Your friend's father lost his job and now the friend cannot go to camp with you.
11. A plane crash in Switzerland is announced in a special news brief and a whole family from a town near you was on it.
12. You feel ashamed of your house because it is smaller than all of your friends' houses.
13. There is a boy in your class whom the kids laugh at and the teacher picks on constantly.
14. You and your friends are going on a bike trip. When you go outside to leave, your bike is broken and nobody in your family can help fix it.

You have probably heard friends and adults use expressions that describe their feelings of helplessness:

"I felt like I was left in the dark."

"It was as though I were up the creek without a paddle."

"I couldn't do a thing; it was as though I had both hands tied behind my back."

"I felt so useless."

And you may be able to help them express their feelings by having other words in your vocabulary that describe helplessness:

hopeless	futile
defeated	powerless
angry	frustrated

Feelings of helplessness may be expressed differently by girls and boys. Boys may try to act as if they do not care, or they may get busy immediately doing something—anything—to avoid thinking about what is bothering them. Girls are more likely to brood over the problem.

Girls and boys need to be encouraged by friends to express in words, openly and honestly, what is bothering them. Otherwise, they may hold unexpressed feelings inside and express them through other behaviors—angry outbursts, sullenness or withdrawing, eating or not eating. Once the feeling of helplessness is expressed by a friend, try to help your friend either *do* something about the situation or accept that he or she cannot do anything about it. And if he or she has tried to solve the problem and failed, let your friend know that the important thing is to try and to do whatever is possible; but that he or she cannot expect to do the impossible. You might point out that something has been learned from the experience that will be useful in the future.

Finding solutions and accepting realities

Girls and boys experience helplessness in similar situations. But there may be some differences when it comes to how boys and girls cope with their feelings of helplessness.

Boys Helping Girls

1. *Lost money:* The girl who lost her money should go to a police station and report the loss. There may be emergency services for such a situation. She might try to contact her parents or a relative by phone. She might also go to a store, look for a sympathetic manager, and ask if there was any work she could do to earn some money—fast!

2. *Divorced parents:* You can assure your friend that it is not her fault. Parents who are very unhappy with each other are probably too busy being hurt or angry to notice how their behavior is affecting kids. After the divorce, she will probably see that her parents are better and that the tension in the house is eased. She may then be able to tell her parents (one or both) how she feels and ask them, when they are calmer, to explain better why they are divorced. This just may take a little time. Meanwhile, she must be reminded by her friends that she is not responsible for her parents' breakup.

3. *Shouting teacher:* You could tell your friend to go

132

to her guidance counselor and explain what is happening. It is very upsetting to listen to someone shout constantly. The guidance counselor may not be able to stop it, but your friend will feel better to have discussed the problem with someone at school.

4. *Messy room:* It's no use feeling sorry for her situation. Try to help her get organized. Offer to lend a hand cleaning her room thoroughly. Maybe she'll find it easier after this initial cleanup.

5. *Nuclear power plant:* If your friend is worried about a nuclear power plant opening in her town, she should get involved in some community effort opposed to it. She might want to do some reading so she is well informed. She could then get the name of a local representative in her town or on a state level and write a letter to express her view. The town or city hall or the state capitol may be able to give her the name of an organization working on the nuclear power issue.

6. *Children starving:* She could go to the library and find the address of a world food organization. If she writes to it, the group will probably have suggestions for how individuals can work on this problem.

7. *No money:* Point out to your friend that she's really not helpless. She could make her mom a present—mothers love handmade gifts! Or she might give her an IOU for something: she could serve her breakfast in bed, or run an errand without complaining.

Girls Helping Boys

8. *Earthquake:* Look in the paper the next night and see if there has been an attempt to organize assistance relief for the survivors. Realize, too, that in expressing his feeling of helplessness, he may also be covering other feelings: he may be wondering what he'd do if *he* were ever in an earthquake. He may want to talk about this feeling of fear and personal helplessness too.

9. *Dog mistreaters:* If his neighbors are mistreating their dog, he should do something about it. He could

go over and tell them how he feels about what they are doing; maybe they do not know how to take care of a dog. If they continue to mistreat the dog, he could report them to a humane society or the dog warden in town. Or, he may have to accept what they are doing, but he could give the dog extra food and attention himself.

10. *Unable to go to camp:* If his friend is unable to pay for camp, he may just have to accept the situation; this may be sad and difficult for him, but he may not be able to do anything to help. It is possible though, that he and his friend (if they have time) might try to figure out how they could earn the money together. He should also remember that if he is feeling bad about his friend not going to camp with him, his friend is feeling worse. If there is no way to help, then he should at least not make his friend feel worse by talking about how much fun camp is going to be. Also, he could consider not going to camp and instead finding another activity that they both could do.

11. *Plane crash:* Your friend is probably feeling helpless thinking about the family of those killed. He is probably also identifying with how it must feel to be utterly helpless in a plane that is crashing. He may just need to talk about how he is feeling.

12. *Ashamed:* It is really too bad if your friend is ashamed of his house. Obviously there is nothing he can do about having a house smaller than those of his friends. What he can do is to change his feeling. You and his other friends like him because of who he is, not because of where he lives. Also, everyone knows that parents control where kids live, not the kids. If your friend has his own room, he can do things to his environment to make himself feel good about his special space; mostly, however, he should know that real friends will not judge him by his house.

13. *Feeling sorry for boy:* Watching a person get picked on constantly is very painful. Your friend may

not be able to make the other kids or the teacher stop, but he can make a special effort to be friendly to the boy himself. He can go out of his way to talk to him and walk with him into and out of the room. This will certainly make the boy feel good, and maybe the others will notice and begin to change their behavior.

14. *Broken bike:* If this happened to your friend, he must have felt totally helpless. You could help him by sharing a disappointment you may have had, or by offering to do something with him since he could not go biking with his friends. You could also let him know that if something like that ever happens again, he could call you and you would lend him your bike.

Learning to recognize helplessness

Case Study

It is Thursday, and at school today James ran into difficulty with his science teacher and the vice-principal. It seems that Ralph, the fellow who sits behind him, threw a piece of chalk and hit Alice on the head during class. Alice spun around and saw James laughing. She then accused James of throwing the chalk. James denied it. The science teacher took Alice's side and no matter how much James said he was innocent, neither believed him. And James did not want to tell on Ralph.

At this point James feels helpless. Since he will not tell on Ralph, he may have to take the punishment for the act. The science teacher sends him to the vice-principal's office, and she doesn't believe him either, creating more of a feeling of helplessness. James needs to gain some control so he puts on the mask of anger and directs it at the vice-principal, who in turn gives him detention for one week. She also gives him a note to take home for his parents to sign that tells them why he has to stay after school.

James is now feeling anger at the two adults in the situation and is sure his parents will take his side when he tells them the story. On his way home he is really boiling mad. He starts to think what will happen when he gets home. His mother will be there and he will explain calmly what happened in school. She will call and make an appointment for tomorrow and straighten it all out. School does not close until 4:00 so she will have plenty of time.

When he gets home, no one is there. He remembers it is Thursday and his mother and father always go shopping and out to dinner on Thursdays. They will not be home until 6:30 or 7:00 P.M. Now he starts to get mad at them because he thinks, "They are never here when I really need them." They arrive at 6:45, and by this time James is fuming. He yells at them for not being home. "Why do you have to go out every Thursday?" His father reacts angrily and grounds him for the weekend. His mother is upset, because she actually feels that it is her fault for not being home.

———

Now let us look at what happened and how James handled it. James came home feeling angry, when his original feeling was helplessness. His anger was his way of protecting himself from his feeling of hurt for being unjustly blamed for something he did not do. As for his parents, they did not know what happened. They did not plan deliberately to be away when he needed them. Yet he was treating them as if they had abandoned him.

If James could have calmly told them the story when they arrived, and if he could have told them the truth—that he had felt *helpless* with the vice-principal and science teacher because they were authority figures—things might have ended differently. His parents could have seen what he needed. But James feels it is wrong to feel *helplessness*, because it takes away his masculinity—males must be in control. He is much more comfortable feeling angry and tough.

Why do males wear masks more often than women? Is it true that society allows females to be more emotional and dependent? Are boys truly not allowed to feel emotional and dependent; have they been taught that to feel emotional is not masculine? Males in our society are given ideals when they are very young, and they spend the rest of their lives trying to live up to those ideals. Traditionally, one of those ideals is that

137

men must never feel helpless, insecure, uncertain, doubtful, or vulnerable.

This is changing for boys today—not by leaps and bounds but gradually and slowly. Boys are being given permission to express their true emotions. In the past, men have had limited roles; now these roles are expanding. It is not unusual to see fathers pushing baby strollers, doing the grocery shopping, becoming nurses, or being not the major but the secondary breadwinners of their families. Boys do not have to always "act like a man"—strong and silent and always in control—to be considered manly.

Divorce and feelings of helplessness

Case Study

Martha is twelve years old and thinks that her mother and father do not consider her feelings and problems. She feels as though she has been left in the dark. Her parents have recently gotten divorced, and Martha says she has no idea why. She now lives with her father and often feels as though her mother has deserted her. Her mother had wanted a career and her father opposed it. He said that Martha needed a full-time mother. He shouted that that was the way his parents did it and that was the way it was going to be done in his family. After her mother began to work, the daily arguing and tension intensified. His arguments were still one-sided. This may have been one of the reasons for the divorce. Martha often complains about feeling like a ping-pong ball, going back and forth between her parents' apartments. She feels that her parents are competing for her affections.

Her feelings of helplessness come partly from her inability to say what she wants because she is afraid of losing the love of one or the other parent. She also feels helpless for another reason: she wants to invite both of them to her basketball games and feels caught in the middle. She feels torn when her father says, "If you are going to invite *her* to the games, let me know and I'll stay home." So she does not invite her mother and again she feels helpless because someone else is making a decision that should be hers. She says that her father "just doesn't understand." Martha is afraid to be too assertive because she does not know how her father will respond; she thinks he will either not listen or become very angry.

———

Martha is in a difficult situation that may seem impossible at times. There are ways, however, that a friend could both help her cope with her feelings and offer concrete suggestions to help her overcome her sense of helplessness. Here are some suggestions a friend might give:

☐ Martha could ask each parent directly to tell her the reasons for the divorce.
☐ She could explain why it is important to her that both of them be at the games.
☐ She could take turns inviting each parent separately to alternating games. She could also do this with other school and social occasions like school conferences, concerts, awards dinners, and movies.
☐ She must realize that she cannot control or change her parents. She cannot make them be comfortable with each other. She must decide how she can gain control of certain situations and take charge of directing those times. She will feel sad at times, but she will overcome her feelings of helplessness. She will define more clearly her own emotions.

Many people, like Martha in the case study, have experienced a divorce. If you have a friend whose parents are separated, are getting a divorce, or have been divorced for a while, you may wonder:

1. Does she miss her parent (mother or father) who does not live with her every day any more? What is it like when parents are divorced?

Most kids would say, "Yes, sure, I miss the parent who doesn't live with me every day. But you do get used to it, even though it takes a while." You may continue to miss your parent, but you probably stop thinking that he or she should live with you in your house again. And, although you gradually feel more comfortable about seeing him or her only one or two times a week or month, often you leave wishing you could have stayed longer. And you may occasionally wonder if you and the absent parent will ever live together again, or if your parents might somehow get back together again.

2. Why did her parents get divorced? What was it like before they were divorced?

There are different reasons for every divorce. The most universal, common reason is that the parents do not get along with each other anymore, and they no longer feel the kind of romantic love for one another that they did when they were first married. Some parents still care about each other; they worry if one or the other is sick and may acknowledge special occasions like birthdays. Other parents are very angry or resentful and have a lot of difficulty talking to or seeing each other. The important thing to remember is that the parents may not love or even like each other anymore, but they still love their kids.

Some kids feel better when their parents get separated because there was tension and arguing every day before the separation. Other kids are surprised to find that they feel better; they had not known how unhappy their parents were; they never heard much arguing or fighting. The parents tried to keep it from them, yet there was a lot of tension in the air. And other kids feel angry because they did not sense any problems and had no idea how bad things were. They feel guilty when they think back to the time before the divorce because they think they should have been able to see that one or both parents were so unhappy, and somehow prevent the separation.

3. Does she ever get mad at her parents?

Sure! But most kids are only angry at their parents (and the world) about the divorce for a while. (Some kids are not angry at parents for getting divorced, but are upset by the changes that follow.) After a time, kids are angry at their parents now and then for the same reasons all kids get mad at their parents occasionally.

4. Does she think or hope that her parents will get back together?

Some kids say "yes" for a while during the first part of the separation. Other kids say "no, never!" Do not be surprised if girls seem more willing than boys to discuss these feelings with friends. Boys and girls agree that it is good to be comfortable about telling friends how they feel, if and when friends ask; but boys tend to ask fewer questions and are less inclined to discuss their inner emotions.

5. What should you say to her on the day the divorce is final? Will she want to be alone or will she want company? Will she want to talk about it or not?

To most kids, the more difficult time is when the parents first separate rather than the day the divorce is final. When parents are first separated, kids need to know what to say to friends. Close friends can help by not being afraid to say:

□ Where is your dad (or mom) living now?
□ Will you be seeing your mom (or dad) on a certain day or on weekends?
□ Can you call your dad (or mom) when you want to?
□ Does (a mutual friend) know that your parents are separated? Are you going to tell them? What should I say if they ask me?
□ How is your mom (or whichever parent is away from home)?

Kids should keep doing all the things they have done before the separation, like going out with friends and staying overnight at each other's houses. Kids whose parents are just separated want to know that other things in their life can still be regular. Later on, they will come to terms with the fact that their household and family is different from the way it was before—but still normal.

If you have a friend whose divorced parent is getting remarried or is remarried already, you may wonder:

1. What is it like having a stepparent?

This depends on several things, such as the individuals and their personalities, how long kids had to get to know the stepparent before the marriage, and whether the stepparent has kids.

2. How else will this change his life?

When a parent is going to remarry, the biggest question is who is moving where? Until this is worked out, kids will feel anxious. After this is worked out, kids face a period of adjustment. It may mean a new neighborhood, a new school, different responsibilities in the house, and different rules. It may also mean giving up some familiar comforts and possessions, or acquiring different possessions.

3. What kinds of things does he worry about?

Probably the same things all kids worry about. School is a big worry—teachers, grades, classes, sports, friends—all of it. And in a general sense, he is probably wondering how everybody will get along. Your friend's life now can be a kind of adventure into new territory. If the two adults have decided to marry, figuring out how the rest of the puzzle pieces will fit together usually is more of a curiosity than a major worry.

Some things that parents do or do not do can make

a big difference in how a kid feels about the divorce. If they feel they have to take care of one parent or the other, it is hard on the kids. If one parent does not make an effort to work out plans for time with kids, bad feelings about the divorce (sadness, depression, loneliness, anger) may linger for a longer time. If parents do not invite kids' opinions, kids may begin to feel helpless and this will affect friendships and school work.

Here are a couple of things that can happen:

If you live with your mother and she marries a man with children, it means you have to share your mom with his kids sometimes (whether they live with him or with their own mother full-time). You also get to learn how he is with his children, and this may help you adjust to how he will be as a stepfather for you. Together you are all coping with the new relationships.

If you live with your father and he marries a woman who does not have children of her own, this can be comfortable if she understands kids your age but hard if she does not. She may not have patience with things such as your playing music too loud, or she may not be comfortable with your friends being around the house. You will have to learn how to discuss and negotiate these things.

You and each of your friends live in a family, but today there are many different types of families and a variety of household combinations and living arrangements. The basic family types are the nuclear family, the single-parent family, the extended family, and the blended family. In a *nuclear family* the two parents and the children live together in one household. The *single-parent family* means a family where one parent is in charge of the kids in the household. This kind of family may include a single (unmarried or divorced) parent (usually the mother) living with a child or children; the children here may have no contact with the absent parent. Or this family may be one where the parents are divorced and the kids live primarily in one house but have regular contact with their other parent. An *extended family* means grandparent(s), aunts, uncles, or cousins living with a nuclear or a single-parent family in one household. A *blended family* is one in which a parent has remarried a person who also has children. There are many possible combinations when two families are blended together.

Close friends can help by being understanding about the changes in the family, by being ready to listen when a friend needs to talk, and by accepting the fact that a friend in a new situation may not always know what plans they can or cannot make. It takes time to work everything out.

Fear

Dear Beth,

I'm scared of girls. I never know what to say. When I try to talk to a girl, I'm all shy and my mouth gets dry and no words come out. I'm so afraid I'll make a fool of myself that I just stand there like a big nerd and they give up and go away. I tell myself, "Well, stupid, you did it again!" and I swear next time I'll just say "hello" at least, but the next time comes and I'm just as dumb as ever. How can I get over this?

John the Dumb Ox

Dear Beth,

I have a problem, a problem I can't handle. I'm miserable. I hate my life, I really do!! I feel so unwanted. I don't belong. I'm a girl of thirteen. I get so depressed and guilty over things. I feel as if I've let everyone down—my parents, sisters, brothers, and friends. I don't get along with my father. Everything is going wrong in my life. I can't take this depression. No one knows how many times I've been so *hurt*! I'm scared and feel so alone. Please help!

Scared and Alone

Scared and Alone and John the Dumb Ox are each expressing a kind of fear—an emotional fear about themselves and about the future, a fear concerning their ability to handle life, a fear about the unknown.

Scared and Alone is:

□ afraid of her feelings
□ afraid she has disappointed family and friends
□ afraid because she feels isolated, lonely, misunderstood

John the Dumb Ox is:

□ afraid of girls because they seem foreign (unknown) to him
□ afraid that he will be humiliated or embarrassed
□ afraid he'll never get over these feelings

Beth's responses to Scared and Alone and John the Dumb Ox are at the end of this chapter, so you'll have a chance to think about how you would cope with their problems, before reading Beth's advice.

There are many kinds of fear. Fear is an emotion that is caused by physical or psychological factors. Physical causes include, for instance, fear of being attacked, the fear of animals, or fear of heights. Psychological causes are more difficult to identify; they include fear of failure, fear of criticism, or fear of the unknown. In describing their fears related to threats of physical harm and their psychological fears, boys and girls have noted some fears that are increasing in today's world, along with age-old fears.

Boys may be surprised to hear some of the things girls are afraid of.

"I'm afraid of my brother!"
"I'm afraid of walking home alone—of being raped or mugged."
"I'm afraid of stoves—of getting burned."
"I'm afraid of being yelled at by teachers, and of taking tests, and of missing the bus in the morning."
"I don't like being in the house alone at night."

"I'm afraid of *boys!*"

"I get scared in suspense movies like *Jaws.* I was a nervous wreck!"

"Sometimes I wonder if I have some terminal illness that my parents aren't telling me about. I just think that once in a while—and then I think I'm weird!"

"I get scared when I hear tornado warnings and I'm not home in my own house."

Girls may be interested to hear some of the ways that boys experience fear.

"I'm afraid of my sister! I mean, she's stronger than I am and she can be mean."

"You know that ride at amusement parks where the bottom falls out and you spin around standing up? It's scary, but it's great."

"I'm afraid to say anything or even look wrong at some of the guys in my school."

"In those gory horror movies, I get so scared I think I'm going to die!"

"One year, our class was going to New York City and we were supposed to go to the Empire State Building. I'm really afraid of tall buildings; I worried all night how I'd handle it. Luckily, we didn't have time to go!"

"I am afraid of being rejected by girls."

"I used to be afraid to stay at my grandfather's house alone."

"I panic when I have to stand up in front of the whole class and give a speech."

"I get scared when I'm with the guys and we're fooling around in a store and I think the manager is going to yell at us."

"I'm afraid to try out for chorus, because what if I don't make it?"

Fears on the rise

Since we all watch the news on television or read the newspaper, we are exposed to a lot of violence every day. You may hear that the violent crime rate increased in a certain city: muggings were up 10 percent, rapes up 5 percent, murder up 1 percent. Or you may read about terrorism, assassinations, hijacking.

How does a violent world affect you and your family? You may hear your mother or father say, "See why I have told you, time after time, not to go out alone at night? Look what happened to that person. Now do you understand why I nagged you about that?" If you live in a major city or a high-crime area, you may be saying to yourself, "Oh, wow, I was right where it happened just yesterday." So the news can make you feel nervous and fearful—you worry that next time it may be you. We may be, as a society, developing a general, ever-present anxiety that is always with us.

However, you usually forget about yesterday's news quickly and go about your business. Or you convince yourself that "it would never happen to me" or a similar coping mechanism. Some fears can be reduced by applying common sense; for instance, by walking with a friend whenever possible and by not opening the door to strangers. Your school council might sponsor a poster contest to encourage safety, or begin a student patrol to stop violence and vandalism in school. You need to figure out a healthy way to be concerned and cautious about your own safety and the safety of those around you, without being overwhelmed by feelings of fear and powerlessness about world affairs. We cannot help being affected by serious world problems and crises. But it's more useful to try and channel your fears into action than to panic. You might contact your local newspaper to see if they'd consider a column by kids about world issues. You might want to campaign for a candidate you like, or organize a petition or a letter-writing movement for a particular cause.

Age-old fears

Hurricanes, storms, thunder and lightning, blizzards, tornadoes, volcanoes, and earthquakes—these natural phenomena are not new. We have no control over them. Myths (stories to explain why such things happen) were an early method of attempting to overcome fears and to make the unknown known. Now science has provided us with explanations. Yet everyone still expresses some degree of alarm or fright at natural catastrophes.

You may learn how to react to these situations from your parents' reactions. If your father is very nervous during storms, you may be too. If your mother is calm and reassuring, you can be too. Emotional responses can be learned. Of course, a degree of caution and the ability to take sensible precautions can also be learned, and are advisable. You could take a First Aid course, for instance. But if you always react to a particular event (such as lightning) with extreme fright and panic, you may have to work at developing a calmer response. Reading scientific explanations, and evaluating how your family's reactions have contributed to yours, may help you develop realistic strategies for coping. You may then be able to unlearn your old response and adopt a new one.

Extreme fears: phobias

A phobia is an extreme fear of something that most people have few problems with. Some common phobias are *acrophobia* (fear of high places), *ochlophobia* (fear of crowds), *agoraphobia* (fear of open places), *claustrophobia* (fear of closed-in places), and *zoophobia* (fear of all animals).

When someone is phobic, the fear does not easily disappear, even after someone shows the phobic person that there is nothing to be afraid of. For example, a person may have an unreasonable fear of dogs. You want to show him that your dog is nice and will not harm him. First you tell him your dog is harmless, then you demonstrate it by asking someone else to pet him in front of the phobic person. Your dog responds gently and doesn't growl or bark. In your mind, you may feel that now there is no reason for your friend to still fear your dog. You may be right. Yet you could repeat this over and over and over and over . . . and your phobic friend may still be afraid of your dog and all other dogs.

It is important not to make fun of the fear that someone has, or to discredit it ("How could you be afraid of my dog Sebastian? He's never bitten anyone!" or "You mean you'd never ride in an elevator? That's ridiculous!"). A person with extreme fears usually has to go to a professional counselor to get rid of them or to learn ways of coping with them. Phobias can seriously interfere with daily life, when that which a person fears is unavoidable. For example, it is very difficult always to stay out of crowds, or never to go over a bridge. When phobias are creating continual problems in someone's life, professional help is required. If you find that you are continually terrified by something that no one else seems to be troubled by, don't be ashamed of seeking help. There are many methods available for helping you cope with a phobia.

Common fears

Fear of the Unknown

"What will happen if my parents divorce?"

"What will happen when my parents see my report card?"

"What will happen if my brother runs away from home?"

"What will happen when I transfer to that new school?"

Fears related to the unknown are hard to work on because you have little or no control over what is going to happen. You may have to endure some anxiety until the unknown becomes known. But you can prepare for it by imagining possible outcomes, and by exploring the feelings you are anticipating. You may even know already how you are going to feel or react, but perhaps you are afraid to face that feeling. Sometimes when people are afraid to face their real feelings they experience physical reactions such as stomach aches, headaches, shortness of breath, or insomnia. When they begin to face their emotions, these symptoms often disappear. For example, suppose you are afraid of your brother running away from home. You imagine you'll feel sad, worried, or angry at him. You know you will have to see your parents being upset, and that may make you feel helpless. By getting yourself used to these feelings and practicing possible outcomes in your mind, you may find that although you still worry about the situation, you feel less terrified.

Performance Anxieties

Performance fears are related to your expectations for yourself. You usually have control over your own behavior and over the results of your behavior. But your expectations for yourself are influenced by others' expectations of you. You may want to do well on a test because it means a lot to you; but you might also ask yourself, "Who else am I performing for? My parents? My teacher?" Consider these possibilities:

"If I do not do well on the test, I will not get praise."
"If I do not do well, I'll disappoint my teacher."
"If I do not do well, my parents will be angry at me."

If you feel your parents expect too much of you, you might ask to see your guidance counselor or the school social worker. They might give you suggestions on how to discuss your feelings with your parents or they might suggest a meeting with you and you parents to discuss your feelings.

If you are feeling anxious about your performance on some task, you might consider ways to reduce your fear. One way is to realize that you are probably being harder on yourself than anyone else will be. Others are generally not as critical as you think. Of course, some anxiety before a test or a tryout is natural and healthy. But if you have studied or prepared or rehearsed as best you can, the most positive approach is to relax (immediately before you are about to begin), clear your mind, and imagine that you are completing that task perfectly in an evenly paced, calm manner. Otherwise, your anxiety will interfere with your true ability and you will fulfill your own fears, instead of your best potential.

Another way to reduce performance anxiety is to imagine the possible outcomes, the "what ifs," as you would do when dealing with the fear of the unknown.

"If I don't do well on this test, can I go to the teacher and discuss a makeup exam?"

"If I don't make the team, can I accept the fact that not everyone makes it, and that maybe I'm not quite good enough—this year?"

"If I forget my lines in the play, will I be able to pause, clear my mind, and carry on?"

Performance fears often have to do with our perception of other people's reactions to our successes or failures. It may help if you stop and think about how you'd react to someone else in the same situation. If your friend forgot her lines in the play, you would probably feel sad or sympathetic, and you'd show her you understood—you wouldn't make a totally negative judgment of her or stop being her friend because of it. Friends tend to sympathize rather than criticize, if you have made a simple blunder related to a performance.

Fear of Success

Some people are unable to deal with success and actually fear it:

"What if I do well now? I'm only fourteen—what will they expect at eighteen?"

"Will success really make me happy?"

"Will being successful mean I have to be perfect all the time?"

If you are a girl who fears success you may try to avoid it by playing dumb, feeling subconsciously that if you act helpless, nobody will ask or expect much from you. But this will backfire, because if it's assumed that you can't win at tennis, play a sonata, do algebraic equations, no one will offer you challenging opportunities to improve, or grow, or take pride in your ability. And if a girl has been taught to win boys' approval and attention by bowing out of situations where she is competing with them, she may find that she is, in fact, ignored rather than desired.

If you are a male, you may tend not to choose certain activities and then to say to yourself, "I could have done it if I really wanted to," or "I'm not really interested in it"—thereby avoiding the chance to succeed at those tasks or skills.

If you are successful at doing something, you may

feel a responsibility always to be successful. One way of dealing with success and overcoming your fear of it is to learn not to blow it out of proportion. You may be exaggerating other people's expectations of you; just because you were a great tragic heroine in the school production of *Romeo and Juliet,* people won't necessarily assume you have to be a perfect comedienne as Dolly Levy in *Hello, Dolly.* Family and friends are proud when you succeed—but they won't disown you if you fail.

Fear of Failure

The fear of failure occurs because you don't want to let others down, or because you have experienced several failures and are hesitant to take another chance. Sometimes others (often our parents) have more invested in our success than we do. They may give you that message by saying, "John, we know you won't disappoint us by not passing that exam." What a burden that is! Perhaps they should have said, "John, try to do the best you can on that exam, but no matter what happens remember that we are very proud of you." Try to keep parents' expectations in perspective. If they are truly encouraging you to do well, accept their enthusiasm. If you feel as if they are pushing you far beyond your limits, try to sit down and talk out how you are feeling. Otherwise, the more pressure they exert, the more resentful you'll feel and the worse you will do.

A self-fulfilling prophecy is a prediction that tends to make itself come true. Both the fear of failure and the fear of success can amount to self-fulfilling prophecies. If a person keeps saying to him- or herself over and over again that he or she is going to succeed (or fail), eventually that person begins to believe that he or she will. And that belief helps make the prophecy become a reality. You should attempt to achieve a healthy balance by not overestimating or underestimating your own abilities.

Fear of Change

Many people find it hard to change; they prefer to stick to the tried and true. There has always been some fear connected with change in our society. Progress, new ideas, and other kinds of change have always been threatening to some people. Coping with change without fear can make your life less frightening, since we experience change continually throughout our lives.

People fear change because they don't know what to expect, or whether or not they will like what is now unknown. If you have information to help familiarize you with the new, you can overcome some of the fear of change. Often young people fear the physical changes that take place when they begin to mature from boy to man or from girl to woman, such as voice changes and wet dreams or menstruation and breast development. The major fear is: "Am I normal?" Keep in mind that there is a difference between normal and average. For example, the *average* young woman today has her first menstrual period at the age of 12.6 years. But you are *normal* if you have your first menstrual period either at the age of 10 or at the age of 15.

There will always be changes in our lives; almost nothing remains the same. Getting a new teacher in the middle of the year, entering a new school, moving because one of your parents has a new job, divorce, a new baby in the house—each of these events brings new experiences for you to adjust to. Each experience brings fears and stress, but can also provide growth and excitement.

For boys about girls

How do girls feel and act when they are afraid, and how do they cope with their feelings?

Jittery, nervous, queasy, weak, dizzy, anxious, shoulders raised a little, eyelids and eyebrows down a little—this is how a girl may appear when she's frightened.

"I want to scream but I can't."

"All alone—just all alone—abandoned by everyone!"

"When I'm with my friends and scared, we all cry and scream, but if I'm alone and scared, I'm quiet, real quiet."

It may seem silly to you to be afraid of spiders and snakes; of darkness; or of parents, strangers, or teachers; but for the girl who is afraid, it is very real and serious. You cannot make somebody stop being afraid instantly, nor can you force her to overcome such fears quickly. It helps to show her that you understand, that you care, and that you take the problem seriously.

You can help a friend recognize reasonable fears and develop strategies for coping.

Is your friend afraid of the teacher yelling at her in front of others, humiliating and embarrassing her? If so, you might point out that if the teacher yells at her, the teacher has probably done it to others; friends in the class know this and they will be sympathetic to what she is going through.

Is she afraid that she will be physically hurt by a particular person? If so, advise her to avoid that person if possible. If that is impossible, suggest that she think through her responses so she will be prepared: Will she scream for help, fight back, report to an authority in the school or community? She can also ask herself if there is a reason for her fear of this person. Does he just give her the creeps or does he really have the capacity to hurt her?

Is she afraid to ask a boy out because she fears rejection? The emotion of love often causes special scary feelings. A girl may be scared to let a boy know she likes him. A boy may be scared to talk to a girl he likes. A girl may be scared of what her parents will say about her having a boyfriend, and a boy may be scared about what his own friends will say. Girls and boys may be scared about how to show their true feelings and how to behave with each other either in crowds or when alone. You will read more about these fears and scary feelings in the chapter about Love.

Is she afraid of failing a test in school? Your friend may feel that if she fails a particular test, it means she is a failure at everything. You can help her regain her perspective and reassure her that her disappointment will pass. Her life is not going to be judged on the results of this one test. Her fear of failure may have to do with worrying about disappointing parents and teachers. Maybe you can help her know that she must succeed for herself alone, not just to please others. She may worry about losing their approval, but she must learn that:

☐ She is probably judging herself harder than they would.
☐ Maybe she will lose their approval briefly, but she will survive, and can succeed on her own.
☐ Experiencing minor failures and overcoming the difficult feelings will help her to accept greater challenges (with less fear of failure and more chance of success).

Some girls may have been *taught* to fear when they were small. Little girls often learn to be afraid of risks, of competing, of daring, of attempting physical challenges. Parents usually allow their boy children more physical freedom than their girl children. A boy has more chances to explore and to discover limitations by trial and error; he is encouraged to be independent and to fend for himself without his parents' constant supervision and approval. Girls are often encouraged to be dependent, and they grow up needing parents' (and later friends') approval, rather than behaving independently. If a toddler boy falls down, a grown-up is likely to say, "Get up and try again." If a toddler girl falls, a grown-up is likely to comfort her and discourage her from trying again. As a girl grows older, she will often find it hard to overcome this early conditioning. If you understand why a girl is fearful, you can better help her to unlearn her learned fear without judging her.

Another fear that girls seem to have more than boys is the fear of saying no. Everybody has difficulty saying no at times; we are afraid to let another person down, or we are afraid they will not like us if we say no, so we avoid it. For girls, learning to say no is part of learning to assert themselves. Many girls who have been brought up traditionally have been taught always to give in to others' wishes and desires; they have not learned that they have the right to say no. As they develop self-respect and confidence they will be able to please themselves, as well as others, by choosing when to say yes or no.

For girls about boys

Here are some specific things boys are afraid of—and how they show that they're scared:

It was common in the past for society to expect that male children would not show fear (even when, in fact, they were afraid). Boys were labeled "sissies" if they did not want to fight, play sports, or put themselves in physical danger. Boys were criticized if they did not live up to a "macho" image. Although expectations are changing, and boys are sometimes allowed or encouraged to express their fears instead of masking them with anger or aggression, boys still tend to fear that their peer group won't respect them if they are not daring and adventurous. If three boys are swimming and one suggests jumping off a really high cliff, one of the others may be afraid to jump, but even more afraid to say he does not want to. For some boys, admitting that they are scared in front of friends is just too difficult. It may take more courage to say, "No, I don't want to," than to do the act itself. Though many boys joke about and even put down the macho image, almost all are affected by it. Some of their joking about it may indicate their anxiety.

According to the stereotype, a macho man must:

- ☐ wear a leather jacket
- ☐ be a jock and play hard
- ☐ be experienced sexually
- ☐ drink hard, smoke cigarettes, swear a lot

A macho man must never:

- ☐ read a book in front of others
- ☐ fail to open a door for a lady
- ☐ listen to folk music or poetry
- ☐ date a girl who is smart or strong

Most boys clearly do not feel the need to live up to quite such an exaggerated macho role with girls. Yet they often do believe that they must always be strong, decisive, and in charge. They secretly fear that they cannot possibly meet the rigid expectations of this role; this hidden fear affects their behavior. They may be overly shy with girls or they may seek a secure sense of identity by attaching themselves to a group of boys. A boy may say to himself, "It's safer in a group. No one will notice if I'm scared, or they'll just think I'm okay because I'm one of the guys." Many boys are afraid to risk being themselves, even if they feel intimidated by the peer pressure in a group. Although most girls don't expect or want boys to be macho (and most boys don't really want girls to be passive and helpless), sex-role expectations will change only when both girls and boys reinforce the positive changes in each other. A girl can do this for a boy by:

- ☐ Opening the door for a boy.
- ☐ Letting a boy know she think's it's cool not to smoke.
- ☐ Complimenting a boy for being independent ("I really think it was great when you refused to tease Marvin when everyone else was doing it the other day").
- ☐ Beginning conversations with phrases like: "How do

you feel about" or "Have you ever been afraid to" or "Let's both figure out how we can get to the dance."

Boys need to encourage each other to feel more free to break away from the stereotype. They need to let each other know that it is okay to cry; to be sensitive and caring; to express disappointment, sadness, helplessness, or fear.

Some boys will put themselves in physical danger on purpose because they are ashamed of their fears and want to prove themselves. Some boys even think girls will like them better if they are tough. To change these ideas, girls must be supportive of boys when they say no to unreasonable danger ("You know, it took a lot of guts not to go hang-gliding with crazy Eddie").

Boys are also often confronted with the dilemma of choosing not to do something they know is illegal or harmful to somebody else. A boy may be afraid to say no to his friends when they want to vandalize the school or shoplift. He is rightfully afraid to do these things because they are wrong, and because he will be punished if he is caught. Boys need to stand up for what they really believe in these situations, without worrying what anyone else will think ("You guys can go ahead, but I don't think stealing is for me," or "I

know it sounds like fun, but I'm not willing to risk getting arrested just to try some new drug").

Boys also have some of the same fears that girls do. They may be afraid of the dark at night, of strange dogs, or of staying overnight at a friend's house. Girls need to realize that no matter how much boys pretend they are not afraid, they too experience fears.

Beth replies

Dear John,

Almost all of us are afraid of the unknown, and the cure is to get familiar with it. Unfortunately, boys and girls are treated so differently during childhood that they grow up thinking of each other practically as enemies. The worst thing you can say to a boy, for instance, is "You throw like a girl." So when boys and girls are supposed to get together as teenagers, many kids feel afraid. The prospect of getting really close, maybe even physically close, is positively terrifying.

Take one step at a time. The truth is, girls are like boys in more ways than they are different. You share many similar experiences—school, friends, teachers, television, music, recreation, etc. So next time, begin a conversation with a girl as you might with any friend, by asking something such as: "What did you think of the math homework?" or "Doesn't Mr. Ryan give you a pain?" or "Did you watch 'Fame' last night?" She'll probably reply, and then ask you what you think. Tell her if you agree or not, and why, and then ask a follow-up question: "I really like that show. Do you watch it every week?" You're on your way. It doesn't hurt to think up a few questions ahead of time, so you will have the ammunition when you need it. After a few exchanges like this, you'll find things *much* easier. But you have to *make* yourself start.

Beth

■

Dear Scared and Alone,

The way you are feeling—miserable, unwanted, disagreeable, depressed, guilty—may be a feeling that will gradually go away when school ends, when the seasons change, or when you suddenly have a good experience or positive event in your life. But right now you do feel alone, and the *scared* feeling comes from not knowing why you feel so down. You may be afraid because you think it will never end. It will end, but you may have to work on it. Here are some ideas you might try:

You mentioned you feel you let your parents, sisters, brothers, and friends down. When you're thirteen it's confusing to know just what people expect of you. Some days they may treat you like a child, other days like an adult. And sometimes you may feel like (and want to be) a little kid, and sometimes you may feel and be more mature. That's natural. The transition from childhood is usually not a smooth, one-way road uphill. You may be feeling so miserable because you're not sure where you are just now.

You mentioned not getting along with your father and this, too, may be related to the changes you are beginning to go through. He may not know what he expects of you now as you are maturing. You may have to make an effort to communicate with him about how you're feeling. Perhaps you could talk with your mother about how you're feeling.

You say no one knows how many times you've been hurt. And that may be very true. You may have to tell people when or why you've been hurt. We often expect others to read our minds, to understand us, when really that may be impossible. Try explaining to your brothers or parents. For instance, if your feelings are hurt because no one complimented a meal you prepared, say: "My feelings are hurt." Little hurts can add up to big feelings—like the depression you describe. You will not feel so scared if you can begin to understand why you feel as you do.

Beth

■

Scared and Alone used words like "unwanted," "miserable," "depressed," and "hurt." They may be the words of someone who needs good professional help.

She should ask someone she trusts for advice about where to go for this kind of help. She could ask her teacher, guidance counselor, or even the parent of a friend.

The size of a community often determines what counseling services are available. If you live in a major city, look in the Yellow Pages of the phone book under "Counseling." A hospital emergency room will have a psychiatrist available. Many towns and cities have an information line where you can call and ask where someone your age can go for counseling. If you live in a small community there is probably a person connected to a community service agency, such as a Family Counseling Center, a Human Services Department, or a police department. Or you may have heard of a clergyman who has helped others, whom you might call. The important thing is that if you are feeling so overwhelmed that you can't begin to help yourself, you should seek outside help.

If you have a friend who uses words like the ones Scared and Alone used, don't ignore his or her unhappiness. Encourage him or her to try and get help, and try to be supportive and comforting by listening to your friend talk about it all.

Confidence

Dear Beth,

I have been trying to get on the track team for two years. The high-school coach said if I worked hard this year I should have a chance. So I trained all summer, and this fall I made it! I was so happy. I guess maybe I talked about it too much or something, because now my friends are saying "You think you're so great." They rank me down for being stuck up about it. I really don't think I am. Isn't it okay to be a little proud about something you have done?

Not Sports Snob

■

Dear Not Sports Snob,

Yes, it is. When you have worked hard and really accomplished something, it would be unnatural not to take pride in it. It is healthy to feel good about yourself when you reach a treasured goal. We all need the self-respect that comes from feeling competent and capable.

Pride is not a matter of feeling better than other people, but of taking pleasure in one's own achievements. If you can only feel good about yourself when you have beaten out everybody else—got better marks, made more friends, won more games, etc.—then you really do seem to be conceited. The funny thing is that people who constantly have to prove themselves this way really do not have much pride in themselves. Basically, they feel they have not measured up and keep matching themselves against everyone else to prove otherwise.

When you strive for something, however, such as

making a team, and you succeed, you should feel happy about it. Of course, a certain modesty is a good thing. Raving on and on about one's success is in bad taste and is boring. But good friends usually feel happy about each other's good fortune. Perhaps yours were disappointed and had hoped to make the team themselves, so they were a little jealous of you.

Beth

■

Dear Beth,

My brother and I and two other guys have been singing together a long time. I think we're pretty good! We even wrote some of our own songs, which aren't too great yet, but they're getting better. This winter we have been asked to sing at two public appearances, and now they want us to perform at the Homecoming Ball. We sing mostly pop-rock, and I feel really good about the way it's working out. The only problem is, the rest of them don't want to sing our songs, and I think we ought to. It's more original that way. . . .

Henry W.

■

Dear Henry,

I enjoyed hearing about your singing group; it's wonderful when you have developed a talent you feel good about. I think you're right—singing your own songs is unique and original. But if the other boys are unsure, perhaps you can compromise by singing some known songs and some of your own. You obviously have confidence in yourself as a composer and as a performer, and that is fine. It may take the others more time to develop a stronger belief in themselves. Meanwhile, you can continue to compose and to improve and practice your original work. Learning to work cooperatively and successfully with each other, especially in a creative endeavor, is very demanding. One must learn to be patient, to compromise at times, to negotiate, and to help build one another's strengths. In the end, the rewards will make it all worth the time and the effort.

Beth

Everybody experiences joyous moments during life. These moments form memories that people hold throughout life. If you think about times when you have felt just plain good all over, you may be recalling moments of happiness or *confidence*—moments when you felt great inside because of a particular accomplishment. Or, you may be thinking of moments when you felt good—just to be alive.

If you were to describe a moment of happiness or pride, you might say that it was a time when you felt:

elated	independent	satisfied
strong	joyous	courageous
pleased	brave	confident

You might be describing a time when you felt wonderful about something that you had earned or accomplished, or about something that somebody very close to you had achieved. Such happiness may come from personal accomplishments or from those of a family member or a friend. You may feel proud about brief episodes with friends and family at home or socially, or about special events at school or outside your family.

You may have had moments when you felt confident or happy that are similar to the moments several girls described:

"Last year I wrote an essay; when my teacher asked me if she could enter it in a state contest, I felt really great."

"I was so proud when I got my first babysitting job."

"I was in a concert once, and my father came dressed in a three-piece suit. I was so proud to have all my friends see him."

"My brother won the state wrestling championship and everybody was calling our house all night. It was terrific."

"Last summer I learned to take my bike apart and fix it. It's neat to know how to do it."

166

"I'm president of the seventh-grade class. I don't want to sound conceited but I am really proud."

"Most of my friends' mothers don't work outside the house. I used to feel so proud that my mother did."

"When I lost the five pounds I'd gained on vacation, I felt so good about myself."

"I came in second in the final gymnastics competition. I felt fantastic! I know it would have been great to come in first, but I was so sure I'd messed up, just being in the finals was wonderful."

"Sometimes adults tell me I'm pretty enough to be a model. I feel so proud but also I'm embarrassed and don't know what to say."

When boys are talking, you may almost be able to feel the pride and confidence they're feeling:

"When I got a job at this beach club near our house, I felt super."

"When I was twelve, I won first prize in an art contest at the library for a drawing of this boat. I thought it was a pretty big deal!"

"When my sister was in the eighth grade, she had to make the graduation speech. I felt so proud of her."

"When our team won the state championship there

Now, that's really something to be proud of!

were articles in the paper and pictures, too. It was great."

"When the manager in the store accused me of taking something I didn't take, I felt so good that I didn't get angry or upset. I just stayed calm and explained—and it worked!"

"I got a mini-bike for my birthday one year. I was the only kid around with one."

"When my father was on the news one night, I was so proud!"

"I taught myself to sail last summer. I just went out every day and figured it out. I felt pretty good about that."

"I was asked to be in charge of photography for the yearbook. I didn't even think anyone knew I could take photos. I was really flattered—and surprised."

"I learned to cook Chinese food at my friend's house. It's really fun, and now I can cook for my whole family."

"We had a foreign kid staying at our house once. I showed him all around and tried to explain things to him."

Kids who experience the good feeling of confidence are developing pride in their abilities and relationships. They tend to be happier, to be good to have as friends, and to enjoy school and other activities more.

Kids who don't have a sense of confidence in themselves and what they can do tend to seem "down" a lot, have little to offer in friendships, and are not happy about school or other work or play.

People begin to develop confidence in themselves when they are children. When you bring a drawing home in first grade, a parent may praise you and tell you how wonderful it is. This happens over and over with other accomplishments, and becomes a motivation for you to continue to try hard and do things well. Teachers, grandparents, neighbors, and other adults also help by offering praise and support for your efforts. Eventually, a person derives a sense of confidence that comes from within—a basic knowledge that they are okay, even if they may make mistakes or misjudgments once in a while. By adolescence, we no longer need constant recognition from others to feel good about ourselves, although compliments and praise and support continue to feel good (and are important to everyone) throughout life.

You may occasionally experience times when you simply feel good and happy for no particular reason. These experiences are also important. They are unexpected moments of contentment or peacefulness which form happy memories for later years.

"I remember a rainy afternoon in a cabin in Maine. We just sat around all day reading and playing games. I remember a day when I was riding my bike, just by myself. It was a beautiful day and I just sort of felt happy to be alive."

"One day I made a cake for this old woman down the street. When I brought it to her house, she cried! To see someone cry for joy because of something I did made me feel very special."

Helping yourself feel good

Today, more and more people are discovering that being active helps them to feel good physically and mentally. There seems to be a sport that is right for just about every individual. It can be an organized sport or an informal activity.

Through sports people derive strong positive feelings about themselves and about others, such as the following:

Comradeship. You may enjoy a sport where teamwork is crucial to success, or you may enjoy going off with one or two friends camping or fishing. The good feelings of friendship and mutual trust mean comradeship—a strong bond between you. Comradeship means developing your strengths and compensating for your weaknesses in a relationship with others who are doing the same thing.

Achievement. There is a great sense of achievement and accomplishment when you have worked hard to perfect a skill like wrestling or to negotiate a difficult skiing maneuver—only you can *know* how good you feel inside.

Physical well-being. Getting in shape, developing endurance, pushing limits, testing, learning what a body can do are exhilarating: "When I finish jogging I feel really high—euphoric—fantastic!"

A good self-image. "I'm a healthy, strong, capable person. I like the *kind* of person I am and who I am. I like what I'm doing and how I'm doing it!" Individual and team sports can help a person develop these good feelings.

Individuality. "This is *me*—an individual; a unique, ever-changing being." Jumping rope, roller-skating, skateboarding, running, and dancing—the possibilities for inventions and innovations are endless. These offer us chances to grow and to expand.

Competition. Will and determination, a fighting spirit—for some, a sport is not a sport unless they are competing. Competition with one opponent or with a team (or with oneself) can feel good and is usually healthy. But if a person's only goal in participating in a sport is to compete and win, it becomes a *battle.* This person usually experiences more anguish than joy in the activity.

Fun. Laughing, relaxing, and just plain feeling good are all part of sports. A sport can balance the pressures of school, home, or work.

People also develop strong positive feelings about themselves through creative endeavors. You may already know what makes you happy, or you may be searching. It is important to find some activity you enjoy.

SHANNON   Thinking out loud; searching for the right word; getting frustrated; and then suddenly knowing it is right—just right—that I am communicating an idea or creating an image with others.

JEFF   It feels good to do something I'm good at. I love the guitar—even if now it's mostly just my family who ask me to play. If I'm ever good enough, I'd like to play with a jazz group.

NINA   I enjoy singing because it's something I do alone and yet something which connects me with others. I like thinking about the great women singers I know.

CHRIS   The more skill I develop, the more I like sewing. Now I can occasionally modify a pattern or design something completely new.

TOBY   I began to draw when I was little. Now I'm studying painting and silk-screening on Saturdays and learning to create my own images.

BRAD   At school, time drags sometimes. But when I'm in the darkroom, I'm never aware of the time. I can work for hours doing what I want to do.

WENDY   Acting is a challenge. First, disciplining myself to learn the lines. Then trying to perfect how I'm acting them, rehearsing over and over till I get it just right.

PAUL   When I'm sitting at the pottery wheel, I'm so relaxed. I think it's like meditating. I just started, but I think I'm going to stay with it.

CAROL   I used to worry that I wasn't really talented at anything. Then I realized that friends often came to me with their problems and one of them told me, "You're such a good listener." So now I know I have something special to offer—I can be a good friend.

You or your friends may have recognized a talent or an interest in something special at a young age. The talent may have been encouraged by family and friends.

However, this interest can only continue to be developed if you possess an inner drive or desire to excel. For some, a talent or interest may not begin until they are older—in high school, in college, or beyond. At first, the persistence and determination that an art or craft requires may be a struggle; you have to stay with something long enough to know if it's really right for you. Frequently, working hard is part of the enjoyment. Enjoying the process itself, the feeling of accomplishment, and the recognition that comes from others are all part of the good feeling that comes from creative pursuits.

If, like Carol, you don't feel particularly creative, don't worry. You may not have stumbled on something that seems suitable, or you may be trying out many different activities. Be confident that eventually you will sort out the best path for you to take—a hobby, a career, or a passion for some subject or activity that will add satisfaction and excitement to your life.

Helping a friend develop confidence

Developing confidence and pride is important to one's self-image and self-concept. If a friend seems to take very little pride in anything he or she does, you can help.

☐ Suggest that she run for a student office and offer to be her campaign manager.

☐ He may have a family member whom he's embarrassed about. You can let him know you think it's neat to have somebody eccentric and unusual in one's family.

☐ Your friend may have a particular skill or talent which she does not recognize as worthy; encourage your friend to recognize it and build on it. Praise is always effective—but it must be honest praise.

☐ Offer to help him copy over his history notebook so he can study for the final exam better. (If he sees

that you think that pride in school work is important, maybe he will think so too.)

□ Ask your friend to play the piano for your parents when she is visiting you.

□ Ask your friend to help you bake a cake for your mother because you know he is a good baker.

□ Let your friend know that you like her ideas for doing a room over and ask her for advice on redecorating your bedroom.

□ Ask your friend to teach you a card game you know he can play well.

No one can feel confident or happy all the time. And because it is made up of so many different details, happiness can be more difficult to describe than unhappiness. Sometimes we take our good moods for granted so that the bad times seem overpowering. Yet, most of us eventually work out a balance between feeling good and feeling bad that fits who we are; we achieve enough confidence to be able to cope with the world. Throughout your lifetime you will be discovering problems and creating solutions. Working through your feelings, in order to achieve a healthy balance, won't always feel comfortable or easy. But by understanding yourself, expressing how you feel, and sharing with others, you will develop a sound basis from which to tackle problems and crises, as well as to eagerly experience life's joys and wonders. The satisfaction you will find in resolving tensions and honest relationships will help ease whatever struggles growing up brings. Good luck!